VINCENT

VINCENT

Duncan Wherrett

First published in Great Britain in 1994
by Osprey, an imprint of Reed Consumer
Books Limited, Michelin House,
81 Fulham Road, London SW3 6RB and
Auckland, Melbourne, Singapore and Toronto.

ISBN 1 85532 330 3

Editor Shaun Barrington
Page design Paul Kime/Ward Peacock
Partnership

Produced by Mandarin Offset
Printed and bound in Hong Kong

Front cover
*The 998cc vee-twin Rapide engine of
1946 launching the new generation of
Vincent motorcycles was smooth and
low revving. The strong exhaust note
was crisp and distinctive. Numerous
components were similar to those used
on the Series A – such as brakes, taper-
roller bearings, wheels, rear suspension,
sprockets, pistons, con-rods, and battery.
Throughout the time of motorcycle
production, every Vincent was given a
specific road test*

Back cover
*By 1959, Nero produced 85 bhp at 6,800
rpm. Compression ratio was 13:1
running on nitro-methane with $1\frac{7}{32}$ in.
GP carbs. There was a seven plate
Norton clutch and a double capacity oil
pump. The flywheel and main shaft
were machined from a solid billet and
mounted in larger bearings. Around
1960, George started testing new slick
tyres with Avon at Gransdon Airfield
and they were soon to become standard
equipment for sprinters. In 1961, the
standing-start kilometre world record
was set at 20.573 seconds and he took
the first British standing quarter mile
record at 10.489 seconds and 85.80mph.
When it was felt that Nero could not be
developed further, George and Cliff
started on Super Nero*

Half-title page
*The cylinders of the 1936 Series A vee
twin were angled at 47 degrees and
offset $1\frac{1}{2}$ ins. to allow both exhaust ports
and valves to receive cooler air. The
standard con-rod could then be placed
side by side on a longer crankpin. A
few cylinders were made of alloy, in
order to save weight, while most were
of cast iron as on the singles. Oil was
fed to the bigends, the rocker bushes,
camshaft bushes and the rear of each
cylinder. The numerous external oil
pipes caused the twin to be dubbed 'the
plumbers nightmare'. A compression
ratio of 6.8:1 and the $1\frac{1}{16}$ ins.
carburettor produced 45 bhp at 5500
rpm. Both cylinder heads were the
same, with the front carb set at a sharp
angle and squeezed under the tank. The
valve lifting levers for the exhaust
valves can be seen, although no cable is
fitted here. Power was delivered
through the four-speed Burman gearbox
but care was necessary in handling the
torque through a clutch which was not
really strong enough for the task*

Title page
*The modified primary chain cover of
the Grey Flash saved more weight. The
small rev-counter was made by Smiths
and was unique to the works machines.
A standard Flash produced 35 bhp at
6200 rpm. Folding footrests and ball-
ended levers have been fitted to comply
with more modern regulations. Works
bikes were sometimes fitted with a
larger TT tank*

Acknowledgements

The author and publishers would like to thank the following people for their generous cooperation in providing motorcycles for photography during the preparation of this book: Glyn Baxter, Sue Barton, Dick Barton, Nigel Bassett, Sid Biberman, James Bridge-Butler, Anthony Brown, Peter Carpenter, Brian Chapman, Jack Charlesworth, Les Cranshaw, Bob Culver, Ted Davis, Bob Dunn, Ray Elger, Alan Elger, Peter Elvidge, Terry Gee, Derek Green, Chris Hayden, David Hills, Eric Houseley, Stuart Jenkinson, David Johnson, Ian Lang, Richard Perry, Ian Poskett, Dennis Price, David Quartermaine, Geoff & Jan Ragg, John Renwick, Bernard Stovin, David Stovin, Tony Summers, Ron Vane, The VOC Spares Co., Tony Wilson, Andrew Walker and Alan Wright. We hope that the result is worthy of your patience.

Although the Vincent was often successfully used on the Isle of Man in the forties and fifties, the handling of the standard machine has made it unsuitable for the higher speeds on the bumpy TT circuit more recently. Chris Hayden built a machine with the Manx TT in mind. Using a 1949 Rapide engine, gearbox and UFM, he fitted Norton forks and the Vincent rear frame was modified to take girling suspension units. Compression ratio was 9.6:1; cams were Mk 2; and the Mk 1 concentric carbs were on extended inlet ports. Chris still had handling difficulties around the the circuit and at times experienced severe weaving and jumping. This he put down to the extreme traction of the racing tyres. These allowed no give and put all the stresses onto the frame. Nevertheless he broke the Vincent lap record with a speed of 92.5 mph, which included a pit stop. Chris's average speed for the six laps was 90.23 mph, while he had also achieved an unofficial lap speed of 96.3 mph. Meanwhile, in the States, David Matson has had numerous record breaking runs on a Vincent over a number of years. In 1985, David was made a member of the Bonneville 200 Club for his mean speed of 202.92 mph. With continuous tuning, in 1988, he achieved a mean speed of 225.643 mph and one run topped 230 mph. (Photo: The TT Photo Shop)

Contents

A 500 Vincent on the track is an even more rare sight than a twin these days, but here is one being raced by Graham Buller at Mallory Park in 1993 during a vintage race meeting. The front fork springboxes have been removed and elektron brake plates fitted

The Early Vincents

From an early age, Philip Conrad Vincent was enthusiastic about motorcycles and was designing machines while still a schoolboy. With financial backing from his father, a wealthy rancher in Argentina, he left Cambridge University early and bought the redundant HRD company for £400 in 1927. Frank Walker, an engineer, was appointed Managing Director and put in charge of finance. With garage premises in Stevenage, Hertfordshire, the Vincent HRD Company began production.

In purchasing the HRD company, Philip Vincent was buying a name with a famous and flamboyant reputation. Howard Raymond Davies started his motorcycle career as an apprentice working for A.J. Stevens, the makers of the AJS. Leaving there to join Sunbeam, Davies had his first ride in the Isle of Man Tourist Trophy in 1914 at the age of 18. A cracked piston during practice meant a new one had to be fitted, which necessitated a slow first two laps. Even so, he finished the race in joint second place in four hours 39 minutes and 12 seconds with an average speed of 48.5 mph. As a pilot in the First World War, Davies was shot down in 1917 and believed killed, but turned up as a prisoner of war. After the war, Davies' employers, carburettor makers AMAC, lent him to A.J. Stevens for the 1920 TT to ride one of their new 350cc overhead valve models. Although Cyril Williams won the Junior for AJS by pushing the machine over the line, the other machines proved to be too unreliable and failed to finish. Significant development work was undertaken to enable the engines to cope with the higher revs on the ohv design and AJS made a determined effort for the 1921 TT. The machines had already proved their worth with Davies breaking several world records at Brooklands and in the Junior TT, Davies finished close behind the winning AJS of Eric Williams in spite of losing 11 minutes with a puncture. After fitting the same 350cc engine into a new frame and wheels, made necessary by the poor condition of the road, Davies entered and won the Senior event – thus succeeding to win the Senior event on a Junior machine.

The following year, TT successes were harder to achieve and Howard Davies became dissatisfied with the machine's reliability. To remedy this, he started building his own motorcycles. Davies lowered the seat and tank as much as the tall long stroke engines would allow, strengthened the frame to reduce any flexing and provided adjustable footrests. Webb girder forks gave better suspension, and larger brakes than usual were used. His JAP powered machines looked streamlined and sporty and caused great

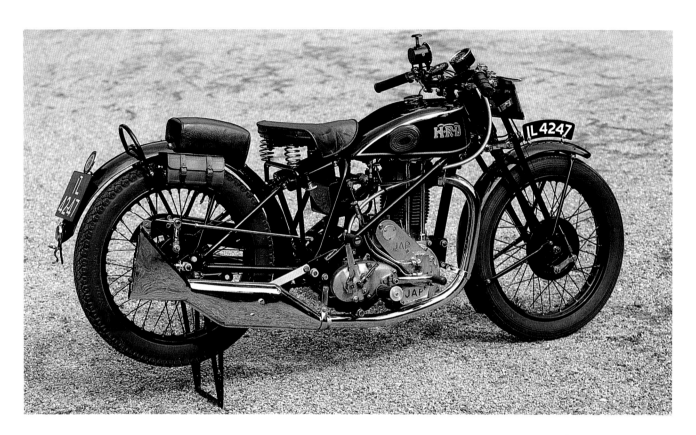

One of the earliest known Vincent HRD machines, from around 1930-1. It features the triangulated sprung frame, which was a patented Vincent design, Druid forks and a 500cc ohv JAP engine with dry sump. The early Vincent HRDs did not have the sleek styling of the previous HRDs, displaying heavy-looking bits of tubing and a 'lumpy' petrol tank. Although the engine internal dimensions are almost square with 85.7mm bore and 85mm stroke, the design of the engine is so tall that it goes right into the petrol tank, thus restricting its capacity to just over one gallon. The carb has to be set horizontally for it to fit. James Bridge-Butler bought this bike as a bit of a wreck in the mid-1980's. The registration was from Londonderry, Northern Ireland, but the machine had never been taxed. The piston was of very high compression and had been run on dope. Much of the frame had been impregnated with salt, which had to be eliminated before new paint could be applied. All this suggests that the bike had been used for beach racing in Ireland. The gearbox was of a later type so James replaced it with as early a Burman box as he could find. Originally, any speedometer would have been driven from the front wheel. Strangely, some of the early Vincent HRDs had the rear brake pedal and the gearchange on the same side. Needless to say, it proved impossible to operate them in a co-ordinated manner when required. Even though the bikes received favourable press reports at the time, this feature was heavily criticised. Two exhaust ports were fitted but one was often blanked off, in fact improving performance. Tapered roller bearings were already being fitted to the rear frame pivot, head and hub bearings. Initially, spokes were attached to the brake drums but this only served to distort the drums, so separate spoke flanges were soon introduced. The oil tank only held three pints and was situated behind the engine. The large diagonal from the front of the petrol tank was soon removed from later frames, but as it is, James finds it an extremely comfortable machine to ride, with good handling and lateral stability.

interest when first seen at the 1924 Motorcycle Show at Olympia. The HRD machines were soon praised for their quality of finish and build. In 1925, Davies came second in the Junior TT and first in the Senior with a record speed of 66.13 mph, consequently becoming a champion riding a machine he had built himself. Davies was never able to repeat his dramatic TT successes, however, and rival firms began catching up particularly by producing their own engines and targeting their efforts specifically at the TT. In spite of some successes around the world the 1926 General Strike, the high cost of the machines and a feeling that motorcycles were too dangerous, meant sales were severely damaged and the HRD company was put into voluntary liquidation.

Following a brief period of ownership by Ernie Humphries, maker of the OK Supreme, it was this name and heritage that Philip Vincent bought in 1927. The first motorcycle designed by Vincent around 1925 while he was still a sixteen year old schoolboy featured a triangular rear frame with springing under the seat and this was to be one of the consistent features of all Vincents throughout their production. Philip Vincent's first machine featured a 350cc JAP engine and a Moss four speed gearbox. It carried the HRD logo and was produced just before the formation of the Vincent HRD Company. Other models soon followed, using 350cc, 500cc and 600cc ohv JAP engines. When first shown, the early machines did not generally impress the public. They lacked the sleek styling of the Davies HRDs and the idea of having suspension on a motorcycle was viewed with definite suspicion.

While Philip Vincent's father was away, his partner in Argentina swindled him out of his ranch and money, which meant extra funds for the motorcycle business were not forthcoming. The 1929 financial crash put a great strain on the company. Fortunately, one of their customers, Bill Clarke, persuaded his father to invest in the business, thus Captain Clarke became chairman and Bill Clarke was put on the board.

In May 1929, Jack Gill left England on a Vincent and sidecar for a world tour. His Model E had a 600cc JAP side-valve engine and, with Walter Stevens as passenger, they arrived in Melbourne, Australia after some nine months. Stevens did not want to continue as passenger and a chance meeting with Phil Irving meant that he accompanied Gill back to England. Phil Irving joined the company in 1931 bringing some new creative engineering expertise into the company. His first task was to tidy up the frame structure of the existing machines and he was to play a major role in Vincent machine development over the next 18 years. With the publicity from the trip, engineers and enthusiastic motorcyclists within the company and extra finance, the position of the Vincent HRD Co. showed good potential.

Vincents were soon producing racing, touring and sports models and

The Vincent HRD Model J was made around 1933-4 with a 490cc JAP engine and four-speed Burman gearbox. Over time, the JAP engines were proving to be unreliable and although Rudge Python engines were better and were offered as an option, Philip Vincent became more determined to produce his own engines. Features introduced about this time included the ability of the rear wheel to take two sprockets to enable it to be reversed for a change of ratios. Also the two wheels were interchangeable and, perhaps for the first time, a motorcycle was fitted with two brake drums. Each brake plate had a hole for the speedometer drive – three of them being blanked off. The rear end of the Model J shows the Vincent Diamond sprung rear frame, with two large spring boxes and a screw adjuster to provide damping. One of the reasons the springs were placed in this position was that there was such prejudice against any form of suspension. It was often felt to be unnecessary and potentially dangerous, so it was expedient to make the suspension as discrete as possible. Large Timken taper roller bearings were at the pivot point. This basic concept changed little throughout the life of Vincent motorcycles and is the usual rear suspension found on most motorcycles today. The rear brakes were operated by a single cable linking them together and running around the rear mudguard. Unfortunately if water entered the cable, it was liable to seize resulting in only one brake working. The brake torque arm and clip changed little in more than twenty years. The support from the rear of the pillion seat to the frame was another Vincent patent. It meant the seat did not move as much as the rear guard and it enabled racers to sit back and crouch. This example has been owned by Tony Wilson since 1956 and was restored in 1973. At the Olympia Show in 1934, Vincents were still the only make with rear suspension and as this particular bike was a show model, it was fitted with chrome nuts and bolts. Of the 33 made only four are known to remain successes on both road and grass brought increased acceptance of his innovative suspension. More than twenty models were introduced between 1928 and 1934 and although in some cases only one or two may have been made, they did provide Vincent with the opportunity of experimenting with new design features. Timken taper roller bearings were fitted to the rear frame pivot; engine and gearbox were fixed to plates to facilitate easy removal; and the balance beam braking system made its first appearance.

A rare bike on the track can be an attractive sight, as is the case with this Model J ridden here by Ann Jenner. The Model J was the first Vincent machine to feature the balance beam front brake mechanism. The beam was prefabricated at this time, and the lugs of the previous twin cable system were still on the machine. Twin cables had the advantage that they were easy to adjust, but the balance beam system provided equal cable forces, offered increased leverage and a more effective brake. It was one of the first models with four brakes. The headlamp and mag/dynamo were by BTH. The engine did not have a primary chain case, only a cover, so a tap was fitted on the return side of the oil feed to drip oil on the primary chain. Lack of sales was a major problem in the early 1930's due to the depression and severe financial position of the country, so as well as offering fast sports bikes, Vincents made other models such as a three wheel delivery van and lightweight machines like the 1933 Model W, which featured a 250cc two stroke water cooled Villiers engine with an Albion four speed gearbox

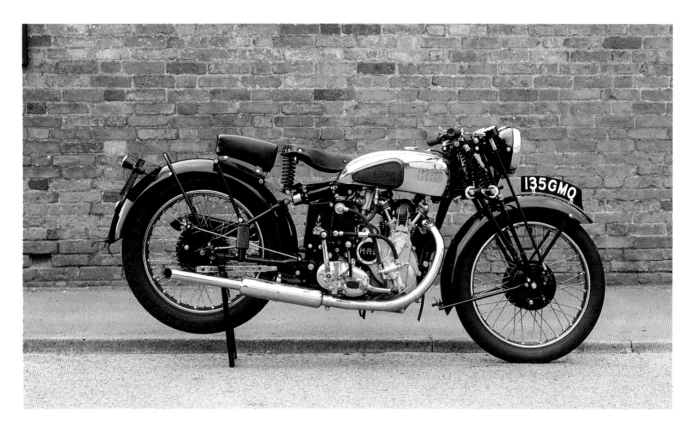

The Vincent HRD Co. went to the Isle of Man for the first time in 1934 and after all three bikes with their new 500cc JAP racing engines broke down, Vincent and Irving set about designing their own engine in earnest. They immediately went for a short stroke 499cc engine with 84mm bore and 90mm stroke, arguing this put less strain on the conrods and it was more convenient to fit a shorter engine into the frame. The high camshaft and mag were gear driven and an external pump provided the dry sump lubrication. The Meteor had 6.8 compression ratio and a 1¹⁄₁₆ in. carburettor, giving 25 bhp at 5300 rpm, while the Comet had 7.3 and 1⅛ in. carburettor and higher lift cams producing 26 bhp at 5600 rpm. A BTH mag/dynamo provided the electrics, with Miller 30 watt mag/dynamos being slowly introduced. The new big-end featured three rows of crowded rollers. The bikes first saw the light of day in 1934. At the time the machines were first shown to the public, Vincent confidently announced that the Comet could reach 90 mph, even though the engines had not even been started then, and that the TT Replica would reach 100 mph even though one had not even been made. Fortunately these claims were soon realised, with the first TT Rep managing 101 mph at Brooklands. Rods were now being used to operate the rear brakes rather than cables which tended to stick if not properly greased. The lower front guard stay also served as the front stand. The Comet Special was a road-going TT Replica with 10TT carb, 8:1 compression ratio, close ratio Burman gearbox and a top speed of 94 mph – even more with a Brooklands silencer. This model from 1937 was restored by Tony Summers. Only 41 were made

Above
The valves and rockers were set at an angle to the camshaft. There were two guides on each valve giving greater stability with the rockers working on a hardened collar in the middle of the valves. This enabled the engine to have shorter pushrods and less overall height than if the rockers were operating on the top of the valves. The Comet Special produced 28 bhp from a 8:1 CR, a 1⅛₂ in. TT carburettor, higher lift cams, lighter flywheels and racing valve springs. The TT Replica sometimes had a shortened barrel to raise the compression ratio and with a similar basic set-up generating 34 bhp at 5600 rpm it could reach about 105 mph. Ignition in this case was by BTH TT magneto. All gearboxes were Burman four-speeds, with close ratios for the Comet Special and TT Replica. The standard cylinder head was made of cast iron but this model had a bronze head because of its better thermal conductivity. The Vibrac con-rod was of 75/80 ton high tensile steel. The outlet from the oil pump had an adjustable union which should provide the inlet rocker with 20 drops per 1000 rpm and the exhaust with 30 drops. The only non-standard item on the motorcycle is the oil switch which contains a micro switch to cut the magneto, so that the engine cannot be started before the oil switch is turned on

Above right
The standard steel tank on the Meteor was finished in black with gold. The Comet tank was usually finished in maroon. The stainless steel tank was an extra £1 at the time and the eight day clock an extra thirty shillings. Four TT Replicas were taken to the 1935 Isle of Man Senior TT and finished 7th, 9th, and 12th. The factory was pleased with the results on what was a new and virtually untried machine. The reliability of the bikes was proved and there was a much needed boost to sales. At the time, Vincents were sold directly to the public in order to compete more effectively with other manufacturers who were usually offering large discounts to the dealers. Vincent experimented briefly with a supercharged model at the 1936 TT but the bulky machine gave a negligible increase in performance and an overheating problem. The supercharged bikes were quickly reverted to normal aspiration but in the mad rush the highest finish of eighth place was disappointing. The factory effort at the 1937 Isle of Man TT was not successful and they did not continue these events, preferring to concentrate on producing road-going sports machines. Privateers, however, were having increased success winning races and breaking lap records

Right
The rear wheel section of the 500cc machines shows many of the design features on much later models – brake torque arms, with quick release clips, rod operated brakes, again easily released by hand, and a tommy bar for releasing the wheel. This meant that the rear wheel could be removed and the chain lifted off the sprocket without the need for any tools. At this stage, chain adjustment required a spanner and the rear footrests were mounted on the frame and moved with it

Above

From 1936, the Vincent powered machines were designated the Series A. After the single cylinder machine the production of a twin of 998cc for effortless high-speed touring was a natural progression and the vee twin was a familiar engine configuration in this period. Numerous parts could be used from the 500cc machine, but obviously new crankcases were necessary. The frame has a longer top tube and a heavier down tube of 1½ inches. Originally tanks were in stainless steel and black; later, stainless steel and red became an option. A pillion seat and eight day clock were also options. The first model shown to the public in November 1936 was very much a cunning dummy and once again Vincent made a confident claim that its top speed was 110 mph. There was always a mad scramble to prepare the machines in time for the shows, but the enthusiasm and spirit of co-operation within the factory was such that the goal was achieved. Production of the finished machines was delayed because the Burman gearbox could not cope with the 45 bhp. After using improved clutch inserts, stronger gears and a stronger casing the first models were delivered in May 1937. The twin was now called the Series A

Rapide and dubbed the 'Snarling Beast' by Bill Clarke. Unfortunately due to the high cost of this hand-built machine and the fact that the 110 mph top speed claim was not generally believed, very few were sold initially. When the Series A twin came out, it was the fastest production machine on two, three or four wheels. 78 twins were made out of a total of more than 800 Series A machines

Above right

The twin's rear end was similar to both the single's and some of the pre-Series A models

The small lever on the primary chain case could be pulled forward and turned anti-clockwise to test the tension of the chain. The tank takes four pints of oil in the left side and 3½ gallons of petrol in the right side. The wheelbase was 56 inches, compared with the 55 in. of the singles. There was a 36 watt Lucas mag/dynamo and the 8 in. headlamp reflector on this model owned by Dick Perry is original. The Burman gearbox, the four plate Burman clutch and the rubber buffers on the clutch sprocket to a large extent were standard components used on other motorcycles

Above

Engine parts for the Series A twin. The large phosphor bronze idler gear was inserted through the slot in the front of the timing case, so the camshaft covers did not have to be disturbed. The external hairpin springs enabled them to be removed without disturbing other components

Left

Known as 'Glitterguts' because of all the chrome, this is the fifth twin ever built. Originally everything was black, and red was never an option. The racing ribbed drums were from the TT Replica. They were a composite drum with the back plate bolted on. The pump can be clearly seen in its place on the front forks. Of the 78 twins made up to 1939, 63 are known to remain

Above
*A smart Series A single at a rally
among more 'modern' descendants*

Right
*A 1938 500 outfit being exercised
during a Vincent Owners Club sprint
meeting with Douglas Stafford and
Rebecca Harrison*

The Series B

During the Second World War, all the Vincent factory effort was directed towards the needs of the conflict. A large amount of new machinery was purchased to service contracts for the Ministry of Supply and other industries. Phil Irving had left the firm in 1937 to work for Velocette and AJS but returned in 1943 to help develop a marine engine for the Ministry. Vincent and Irving continued to create ideas together but it was Irving who completed the necessary drawings. At the same time, they were working on plans for a new high speed touring motorcycle, designed to run on the 72 octane fuel available at the time. The cylinders were now set at an angle of 50 degrees and matched with the Lucas KVF GM1 magneto. Unit construction was favoured because of the increased rigidity, greater alignment of gearbox and primary drive and in order to reduce weight; but an original gearbox and clutch were required to cope with the power and the torque. Another problem was the frame – a conventional frame with a down tube would have lengthened the wheelbase too much. The solution here produced one of the best design features of the new Vincent, although the basic concept had been around for some years. The upper frame member, which was also the oil tank, was a strong backbone on which were attached the cylinder heads. The front forks and the rear suspension spring boxes were also attached to it.

Much of the machinery in the factory was either becoming worn out or unsuitable for motorcycle manufacture. Steel was in short supply after the war and permits were required for its acquisition. The metal might still not be available, or only be allocated to firms who had no work for it. Aluminium was available, however, and this had the advantage of saving weight and reducing the requirement for chrome. As well as new equipment and materials, Vincents needed new skilled workers which all resulted in the company having to commission many components from outside suppliers at the early stages.

The first test bike was ready in the early part of 1946 and considerable testing and development work was undertaken over the next few months. The first Rapide went to a motorcycle show in Buenos Aires in September, 1946 and stimulated tremendous interest and considerable orders. Argentina was to prove a very significant market for Vincents in the next few years. To meet the expected demand, new premises were acquired nearby – the original property now housing the spares and service departments. The new machine was unconventional and eye-catching in appearance. Its power would achieve 0-60 mph in six seconds and a top speed of 110 mph. With

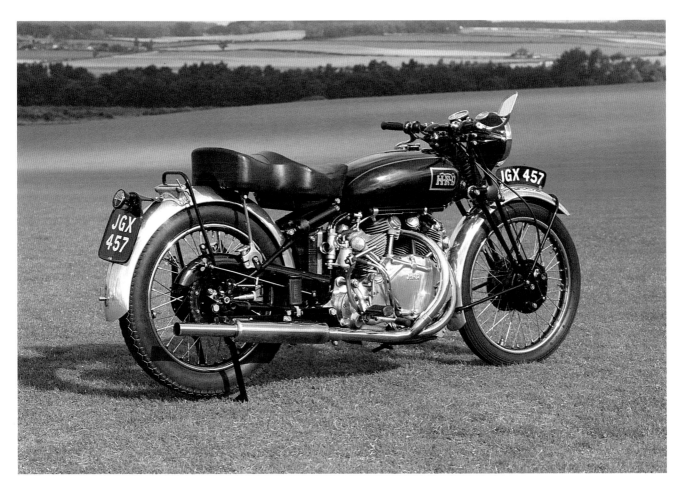

The Series B Rapide was launched in 1946 and promoted with the lines: "The World's Fastest Standard Motorcycle. This is a fact – NOT A SLOGAN." Vincent also used the line "The World's Most Durable Motorcycle" and the more debatable 'fact' – "The World's Safest Motorcycle". With 45 bhp giving a top speed of 110 mph, the Rapide was an exciting prospect for motorcycle enthusiasts after the stark war years. Torque was 53.5 lb/ft at 3900 rpm, so much of the power was at the lower end and hence more useful for normal road use. The HRD initials were still prominent on the tank and embossed on the inspection caps and timing cover. The oil-ways can be clearly seen in the timing cover. The 998cc capacity had cylinders with a bore and stroke of 84mm x 90mm. Compression ratio was a modest 6.45:1 with a 1¹⁄₁₆ in. carb. Standard colour was black with gold lines with badges on the tank and steering head lug. This bike, restored by David Quartermaine, is the sixteenth post-war Vincent to be made, and is the first to have been supplied to a British dealer – all the others having been exported, with one going to the British police. Cliff Brown originally built the engine and the bike was made in December 1946. Dealers were not allowed to sell the early examples as they had to be used as demonstrators. This machine features the original Birmabright mudguards which were stronger than the modern equivalent. The earliest kick-starts had no rubber until the footpiece was redesigned to hold the rubber on securely stability and road-holding to match, the Rapide was soon being used with great success on the circuits around the world. Equally, with a cruising speed of 85 mph and fuel consumption of 55-60 mpg it also met the designers' requirements to be a high-speed touring machine. With the machines being designed and built to a high engineering standard and not to a specific price, the result was an expensive motorcycle, but one which appealed to real enthusiasts. Production difficulties, however, meant that the approximate ten machines made a week was nowhere nearly sufficient to meet the world demand. A coal strike and a national power shut-down caused further delays. New financial backing had been received from the United Dominions Trust; unfortunately their main concern was short-term dividends rather than long-term growth. While Philip Vincent was away for some months recovering from a motorcycle accident, they cancelled the order for the vitally needed new machinery and forfeited the deposits. Vincent was able to change their minds but many months and a large number of sales were lost.

Philip Vincent wanted continuous improvement of the motorcycles and during 1947 Phil Irving and the Brown brothers set about tuning the Rapide into a racer. They lightened the frame, polished the internals and fitted 1⅛ in. carbs, extra valve springs and twin 1⅜ in. 54 in. long exhaust pipes. This marked the beginning of the racing bike soon to be called 'Gunga Din'. Proving to be reliable and fast, and ridden by George Brown, this machine was immediately winning races and breaking lap records in road races, sprints and hill-climbs. In September, 1948, at Jabbeke, Belgium, the bike took the standing-start kilometre world sidecar record at 83.5 mph, the mile record at 94 mph and reached 143 mph as a solo. On a return visit the following year, Rene Milhoux took Gunga Din and a sidecar to a new world kilometre record of 126 mph and but for a blunder with the timing markers would have taken the mile record as well. The Rapide, therefore, at once showed great potential for further tuning and the public was eager to see more. Philip Vincent was also keen to produce a motorcycle capable of two miles a minute – 120 mph. Phil Irving and George Brown began working to this end away from the disapproving gaze of Frank Walker, the sceptical Managing Director. The result was seen in February 1948 in the form of the Black Shadow, offering a top speed of 125 mph. Following this, a wealthy American ordered a machine capable of taking the American land speed record. To meet this request, a Black Shadow, complete with Brampton forks, was very quickly tuned. New high lift cams were made and polished 85 ton Vibrac conrods were fitted. The compression ratio was raised to 13:1 and methanol fuel went through 1⁵⁄₃₂" carbs. The resulting bike was tested by George Brown to 143 mph. As soon as it was unpacked in the States, Rollie Free took the machine up to 148 mph at Bonneville Salt Flats, Utah, to take the record.

Brampton girder forks were used on the first post-war machines. Although most makes were going over to telescopic forks and swinging arm on the rear, Philip Vincent never favoured this system due to its lack of lateral rigidity, particularly with a sidecar fitted. Vincent wanted to give himself more time to develop a new type of front fork which would effectively meet his requirements. The main spring could be 180 or 160 poundage and there was a shorter top link available for sidecar use. The steering damper was adjusted by means of the large bakelite or light alloy knob. A similar knob on the lower spindle tightened friction discs to control the fork damper. The light weight of the girder forks helped provide light steering and the ride was reasonably comfortable. The brakes could be disconnected and tommy bar removed without the need for tools

The designers seem to have got a little carried away with the gearchange assembly. Adjustable for both height and length, it incorporated springs and more than 20 parts. It was complicated and expensive and was soon simplified, and the original version is rarely seen these days. Many early components had the part number stamped on them, as can be seen on the gear indicator lever

Dramatically, dressed only in swimming trunks and lying flat along the top of the bike with his legs stretching out behind, he did a further run at 150.3 mph – this on an unstreamlined, unsupercharged motorcycle. Thus the Black Lightning was born and was to form the basis for numerous record breaking machines.

High speed handling was regarded as superb, with remarkably little vibration. The bottom end was significant here. The large flywheels were made of forged 40 ton carbon steel while the conrods had a tensile strength of 60 tons/sq. in. To help give running with minimum vibration, the flywheels were finished after they had been mounted on the shaft. The standard big-end featured three rows of uncaged rollers, totalling 135 in all. With two bearings on each mainshaft, the flywheel assembly was given considerable support, which all helped towards lack of vibration and longevity. With accurate alignment of the flywheels and the main bearings, it has been quite common for the big-end and the bearings to return a mileage well into six figures, with some examples reaching in excess of 300,000 miles. Very few items were chromium plated, items such as nuts, bolts, footrests and springboxes were cadmium plated due to a shortage of chrome at the time. Today, most owners will use chrome because of its durability

The original rear light with a 'STOP' sign on the casing is of pre-war styling. Being so small the light was not particularly effective, although it was the usual type of fitting for the period. The original three watt bulb and the lack of a reflector would make the standard unit quite illegal today. Six volt electrics were all that was available in the forties and the company opted for the 50 watt Miller unit. Very early dynamos were 3½ in. in diameter with the crankcases having a moulded cradle. This was soon replaced by the 3 in. model and held by a separate holder and clamp

The Vincent had no frame in the normally accepted sense – the engine and gearbox themselves acted as the frame. The oil tank, or upper frame member, was an extremely robust steel unit which was bolted to the cylinder head brackets. The front forks were attached to the UFM via the steering head lug. The rear suspension springboxes and the seat were attached to the rear of the UFM. The two top sidecar attachment points were also in this unit. An interesting touch is that recommended grades of oil were marked on the filler cap. The tank held six pints and the oil left the tank at the rear via an automatic stop valve which cut off the oil once the pipe was unbolted. This meant the pipe could be removed without draining the tank. The oil pressure feed was quite low and with the relatively large feed holes, there was little risk of blockage, especially with the addition of joggle wires. The sump was gravity fed from the oil tank and pumped to each rocker in turn before returning to the tank. A proper circulation of the oil could be inspected through the filler cap. The slow oil circulation meant it could take more than 20 miles for all the oil to completely circulate the engine. With the low engine temperature, it was recommended to give the machine at least 12 miles of gentle running to allow the engine to warm up sufficiently before using higher revs. Very short journeys simply produced condensation in the engine which had a detrimental effect on engine life. Each cylinder was secured by four high tensile steel bolts, replacing the earlier eight hollow and solid bolts. The cylinder head brackets were in turn attached to these bolts and, by means of two engine mounting bolts, the whole engine was hung on to the upper frame member

JRO 102 – the prototype and number one Black Shadow. First registered on February 19 1948 and extensively tested by the motorcycle press, it has been owned by the well-known Vincent names of Ted Hampshire, Alan Richmond and Conways. Its present owner, Bob Culver, bought it in 1978. Philip Vincent had always aimed to have a machine which could cruise at 100 mph, with a top speed of about 120 mph. While he was on a business trip in the States, Phil Irving and George Brown set about tuning a Rapide. Conrods, flywheels, valve rockers, combustion chambers and ports were highly polished and the ports were streamlined. As well as assisting oil flow, the polishing would reveal any small cracks which might develop later. A compression ratio of 7.3:1 and 1⅛ in. Amal carbs all helped to deliver 55 bhp at 5700 rpm. Aluminium engine parts were given a Pylumin anti-corrosion treatment prior to the black stove enamel finish. The black finish on the engine and frame made the bike quite distinctive from the usual chrome and polish. Enthusiastic test reports in the motorcycling press produced a significant start to the sales of the Black Shadow. Performance certainly met expectations, with power delivered effectively through all the gears up to a maximum of 125 mph at 5800 rpm. The large capacity and low revving meant an effortless cruising speed of 100 mph could be maintained at 4600 rpm, while the motor would still run cleanly at 20 mph in top gear. Early advertisements referred to the new model as the 'Black Shadow – Sports Rapide', and about 170 examples were made

Early Series B brake drums were made of pressed steel, soon to be changed for nickel chromium cast iron drums. The Black Shadow saw the introduction of ribbed drums. With the cast iron being a more effective surface for the linings and the added strength and cooling facility provided by the ribs, the brakes became more efficient. Braking from 30 mph was 26 feet. Two shoes were fitted to each brake, and operated by a single cam. Fine adjustments were possible by turning the serrated washer fitted under the cam arm through 90° Aluminium water excluders were fitted on the Vincent for the first time with this prototype. Because the clutch cover could be grounded on fast cornering, a cover with a flat bottom was first used on this prototype. An extra rear mudguard stay was fitted by this time. The early headlamp shell had an 8 in. light unit, soon to be replaced by the 7 in. version. At the time, the lights and electrics were considered good, but complaints soon arose that they were inadequate for the job. This was doubtless true, but it was sometime before the electrics manufacturers were to produce components capable of meeting the night requirements of the faster bikes

Handlebars were almost straight and 25 in. long for solo use. The 5 in. speedometer was specially made by Smiths and was unique to the Black Shadow. It was clear and easy to read and became one of the identifying badges for the machine. The casing for this prototype speedo was made from an aluminium saucepan! Later production speedos had a rounder, slimmer, cast aluminium body. As with the Rapide, the handlebars were finished in black. The twist grip had a single cable with a junction box for the two carbs. Electrics were by H. Miller & Co. Ltd, including the headlamp shell and reflector. The Miller switch and ammeter were particularly renowned for their reliability

Vincent realised at an early stage that there was no proprietary clutch available which could handle the torque the new Vincent bikes were going to produce. The new Vincent clutch featuring a cast iron drum was attached to the primary chain sprocket by six screws and a spigot joint ensured that the drum would not work loose. The action of the single plate clutch operated a clutch shoe carrier and forced the two leading shoes to expand from the centre against the drum. The pressure on the drum increased as the load increased. Slight modifications were made to the early units which improved the clutch's performance. Very early clutches had only three screws on the outer plate. However, if the cable were sticking or the springs became weak, then the clutch became too fierce. A change to six strong springs cured this problem. A one-piece adjuster replaced the earlier component with its troublesome ball bearing. Linings were changed for those with a material which could be degreased. Parts such as the shoe carrier and plate carrier were lightened to facilitate quicker changes. The early long push-rod was changed for a divided rod with a ¼ in. roller. It is a common misconception to regard the clutch as a centrifugal unit. In fact, centrifugal force did not come into

play until revs exceeded 5000 rpm. The photograph shows the clutch shoes before the clutch plates are offered up. Although not standard, six washers have been placed on the clutch plate pins to prevent the inner plate from binding on the shoes. This servo unit was designed to handle 120 bhp, and a although much maligned unit over the years, there is no doubt that a well assembled and maintained clutch would give many thousands of miles of reliable service. The engine shock absorber had 18 pairs of inner and outer springs. This arrangement was regarded as being more effective than a smaller number of larger springs. The chain was triple and endless and the tensioner blade for adjustment was positioned underneath. The case-hardened nickel chrome steel engine sprocket and the nickel chrome cast iron clutch sprocket would show negligible long-term wear. The dynamo drive was taken off the central primary chain above the clutch drum

Right

The new government purchase tax and subsequent price increase created another blow to home sales and this stimulated the move to build a cheaper single cylinder machine. This was a relatively straightforward matter with the possibility of using so many components from the twin. The Meteor was produced as a Series B from December 1948 to February 1950, by which time about 70 had been made. Unlike the Series A singles, the engine was set at an angle of 25 degrees. As with the Rapide, the compression ratio was 6.45:1 with a 1¹⁄₁₆ in. carb and it produced 26 bhp at 5300 rpm. The gearbox was a proprietary item from Burman and was held by a new engine plate and a frame tie which replaced the rear cylinder. With the machine is Ted Davis who joined the factory in 1947 as an engineer

and tester. He was there until 1958 and part of his duties was to test-ride new and experimental machines. He also raced Vincents successfully on short circuits and at the Isle of Man, winning more than 50 national and international races, and was part of the work's team challenging for world records

Above

Regarded as a basic economy Vincent, the Meteor was not fitted with prop stands or magneto cowling. The lower mudguard stay could be used as a front stand as on the Series A machines. With a top speed of 80 mph, the Meteor could return about 80 mpg

In 1934, Cliff Brown joined the Vincent company and was soon followed by his brother George, thus began a long and successful association between the Brown brothers and Vincent motorcycles. During the winter of 1946, George Brown and Norman Brewster built a Series A Comet Special for short circuit racing. George had such success with the resulting machine at tracks like Cadwell and Scarborough that at the time it was referred to as the 'Cadwell Special'. In 1968, Eric Houseley found the machine hanging from a roof in a garage in Yorkshire. He recognised it immediately, having raced against it and George Brown in the late forties. After purchasing the bike, Eric lowered the compression to run it on petrol rather than alcohol through its 1¹⁄₁₆ in. TT carb and shortened the exhaust pipe to increase the top end speed. Eric's son, David, then raced the machine in the early seventies and was unbeatable in vintage races. The plastic bottle for the breather pipe was hastily fitted at a race meeting to comply with new regulations

At the request of West Ham Speedway, London, Philip Vincent, Phil Irving and Matt Wright developed an engine for a speedway frame. They fitted a Series B barrel and head on to Series A crankcases made of magnesium alloy, cast by Birmingham Aluminium. Barrels fins were largely removed on the Speedway models to facilitate a shorter warm-up time. Special shortened bolts were made so that the barrel and head could be removed while the engine was still in the frame. The timing gear was similar to the Series A, although a new camshaft was required to suit the reversed positions of the inlet and exhaust cams on the 'B' engines. Holes were drilled in both sides of the crankcases, to be filled after various holes in the flywheels had been plugged to assist in balancing the engine at optimum revs. The engine weighed a mere 54 lb and produced 39 bhp at 5800 rpm and 39 lb/ft torque at 4500 rpm. The speedway machine had a successful and reliable trial season but the West Ham organisation publicly claimed that they had designed and built the machine. When they also wanted sole world marketing rights, Vincent was not prepared to deal with them further. In all, about twelve engines are believed to have been made and this bike was soon fitted with one of these later engines

The Series C

There was no sudden change from the Series B to the Series C, but a gradual merging from one to the other. The overall concept and design had proved its worth and there was a policy of continued improvement, with changes being introduced as soon as they had been tested and were available. The major change was the move to a new front fork design. The new girdraulic forks were a uniquely Vincent design and entailed a complete disassociation from the telescopic forks so favoured by other manufacturers. Although fairly complicated and heavy, they were extremely robust and had great lateral strength and rigidity – features Vincent regarded as paramount both for sidecar and solo work. Supplies of the new forks were slow in coming through, due to a shortage of production machinery, and machines with girder forks continued to be made for some time after the first girdraulics were introduced. Early motorcycles with girdraulic forks tended to go for export. The new forks incorporated the newly designed Vincent damper, which was also fitted on the rear suspension between the two springboxes. The Series C also saw the re-introduction of the single cylinder Comet – an uprated version of the Meteor. This in its turn was tuned to racing specification and called the Grey Flash. A third road-going twin, following the Rapide and Black Shadow, came in the form of the touring Rapide. As on the Series B version, it featured valanced steel mudguards, wider tyres and higher handlebars. With the racing Black Lightning, five models were available from the factory in the Series C range.

Around the world at this time, Vincents were winning races and smashing track, national and world records. Sceptics who were convinced that the twin would be too heavy, big and cumbersome for circuit racing were soon silenced. At the 1948 Clubmans TT, the standard Rapides comprehensively beat the opposition which included Manx Nortons and KTT Velocettes. As well as coming first, with J.D. Daniels at 80.51 mph, second and in six of the first nine places, ten out of the eleven Vincents finished. George Brown had to push home the last few miles to sixth place after being well in the lead and running out of petrol. For the 1949 TT, the rules were changed to severely restrict the Vincents potential. 1000cc machines were now put in their own race, which was reduced from four to three laps with no refuelling was allowed. In order to achieve even a finish, it was necessary for the Vincents to be detuned with a very weak mixture. As well as restricting the machines performance it also generated overheating problems and risked engine damage. In spite of this, Chris

The Rapide was immediately praised for its steady and stable steering and the ride it provided. It offered a comfortable sitting position for the rider, but some felt the handling was a little heavy at slow speeds. When David Stovin was restoring his Rapide, he set out to make it as standard as possible. He even has such rare items as an original rear light with the serial number stamped on the top, Dunlop rims and an original tyre pump. Dave does admit, however, to not being able to find the small Feridax label which was briefly fitted on the back of the seat. More die-castings rather than sand-castings were used, resulting in the covers for the timing case, kick-start and primary chain case being thinner with a smoother finish. The handlebars should be finished in black. The original Amal levers had no ball ends, while the smaller valve lifter lever was made by Bowden. There was also a separate dipswitch on the left, horn button on the right, the steering damper knob in the centre and twin choke cable levers. The large kick-start crank allows for a good easy swing. A common modification is for the end of the shaft to be drilled and tapped. A 1 in. washer can then be screwed into place to hold the crank more firmly in place

Horn managed a record lap of 85.55 mph – a speed which doubtless could have been bettered without the fuel restrictions. Dennis Lashmar won the Clubmans TT in 1949 but at a slower time than in the previous year, with Alex Philips winning in 1950 at a speed of 78.58 mph. The continuous array of race successes proved the machines reliability and performance, while the factory established world records at Montlhery in 1952. Rollie Free again bettered American record speeds in 1950. Joe Simpson took the mile record with an average 160.69 mph on an unstreamlined Vincent in September 1953, only to be narrowly beaten again by Free, who obtained a top speed of 163.54 mph. Free also took the 10 mile record with 152.32 mph.

In spite of increased demand in 1948, the chairman at the Vincent company refused to sanction the ordering of a much needed production plant. With the resulting shortage of production capacity, the manufacture of the front fork blades was contracted out to the Bristol Aircraft Company. They were extremely strong and were made of forged L40 aluminium alloy with a tensile strength of about 30 ton/sq in. The top link was of a similar material whereas the bottom link was of forged steel. Together with the ⁹⁄₁₆ in. ground steel spindles, these components provided the forks with their unusually high degree of rigidity and lack of twist and were extremely strong in the event of a crash. The new forks provided the rider with secure and steady steering, and with their 5 in. of travel, there was a good degree of comfort. Because the axle travelled nearly vertically, there was less dive than on many other forks. Fork spindles were fitted into Oilite bushes, whereas the non-standard stainless steel spindles and eccentrics available today have helped give the forks a longer service life. The bottom link bracket had two lugs which are not used but were intended for the fixing of a sprung headlamp although the idea was abandoned. The springboxes contained an inner and outer spring each, with just the outer spring on the Comet. The hydraulic damper fitted both on the front and on the rear was Vincent designed and made, and it was a fairly new feature in the late forties. When in good order, the unit worked well but it was prone to leaking. Modifications have overcome this problem today, although some owners prefer to use a modern alternative damper, particularly on the front. The early steering damper had a single friction plate while the later version had two. Over the years, the handling and stability of the Vincent has often been maligned, with the finger of blame being pointed at the front forks. Speed wobbles tended to happen early in a ride, possibly when there was some early stiffness in the damper. There is little doubt, however, that such problems were usually caused by bad assembly and maintenance. With the front damper full and in good order, the damper plates on the steering and on the rear seat stays in good condition and tightened and with the forks themselves kept in good order, the motorcycle would provide a safe and comfortable ride and long life. The usual finish on the forks was black stove enamel

In 1949, the Vincent directors increased the price of the bikes which drastically hit sales. In an attempt to expand American sales, Philip Vincent went to the States and arranged a deal with the Indian Motorcycle Company. A Rapide engine was fitted into the frame of an Indian Super Chief and was referred to as the Vindian. With new engine plates and a pipe on each side, the engine fitted in quite well and sporting the huge mudguards, tyres and American styling, the result weighed more than 500lb. It was said to handle badly and under test achieved a top speed of 100 mph. With the promise of a substantial order and finance from an outside backer, Vincent ordered new materials and castings. However, there was an unrealistically low estimate of the Vincent company's assets and potential by the financiers and the deal fell through. At the same time, the Indian company felt they would prefer to act as agents for the more standard Vincents, feeling they were better and more modern bikes. The short-term outcome was that the company went into receivership and E.C. Baillie was appointed official receiver. Fortunately, rather than just realising assets for the creditors, he took a sympathetic approached and helped the company back on its feet. One move was to lower prices and reduce the large stock of unsold machines, said to be more than 500 at the time. Sales increased, but the company was to remain in a precarious financial state and the real problems of high production costs and inadequate business management were to continue.

With such a well engineered and successful product, it is hard to realise that the Vincent HRD Co. was nearly always in a unstable financial position. Even after price reductions, the Vincent was still an expensive machine with a 1952 Black Shadow costing £389.14s.5d., a Rapide at £347.11s.1d and a Comet costing £274.14s.5d. At the same time a Triumph 650cc cost £220, with rear springing, dual seat and prop stands as optional extras and a Norton Dominator cost £245. Prices were in fact reduced further in 1953, because of improved manufacturing methods and cheaper components, but the main problem was the lack of profitability. The Comet was said to be generating only about £5 profit per machine and observers have commented on the inefficient production methods of the factory. Argentina had always been an important market for the Vincent and Eva Peron had 12 Vincents as her motorcycle escort. Financial restrictions in Argentina, however, put an end to this significant market and severely affected sales figures.

Having joined the Vincent company in 1931, Phil Irving left in 1937 to work for Velocette and AJS. He rejoined the Vincent company in 1943 to help develop the marine engine and finally left to return to Australia soon after the receiver was appointed in 1949. Playing a significant role in designing and developing the Vincent range, he was to become one of the more important figures in vehicle engineering, working on motorcycles,

The standard rear brake pedal was steel, finished in black stove enamel, with a die-cast alloy foot plate. The position of the footrest and the height of the brake pedal were both adjustable. The footrests and the footrest hangers were all made of steel and as well as being strong in their own right, in the event of dropping the bike, they would fold out of the way and usually avoid damage. By using the rear cable abutment on the hanger, the brake pedal could be reversed, thus providing the brake for racing purposes when the rear footrests were being used. The original finish was cadmium plating. It was possible to fit a special kick-start to the left side of the machine to allow a sidecar to be fitted on the right – a unique facility at the time. When not in use, this opening was plugged and its position can be seen in the primary chain case cover

cars and even tractors. In the sixties, Irving designed the Repco Brabham V8 engine which won the Formula One World Championship in 1966. Phil Irving died in 1992 aged 88.

After the 1950 TT and the publicity of the bike's moderate success, prices were reduced by ten per cent resulting in a dramatic increase in sales. During 1952, it was possible to take the company out of receivership. E.C. Baillie was put on the Board and, in further recognition of his significant contribution towards the survival of the company, he was made an honorary member of the Vincent Owners Club. In November 1952, the company name was changed to the Vincent Engineering Co. Ltd, but it was found to be in use already so a month later was changed to Vincent Engineers (Stevenage) Limited.

The Series C gear change was a much simpler design and was no longer attached to the footrest hanger, although the former fixing point was retained on the hanger. With the change from the HRD tank transfer to the Vincent scroll, there was a similar change on the inspection caps and engine covers. A number of items appeared with no name at all in late 1949 and early 1950. This was because the HRD was ground off in order to use up left-over items before the 'Vincent' embossed components came through. The desire to achieve maximum rigidity and compactness for the engine and gearbox meant the designers went for unit construction. Also, at the time, there was no propriety gearbox on the market capable of coping with the power and torque of the Vincent engine. Consequently, Vincent designed their own gearbox and produced a unit that was extremely strong and reliable and easy to work on. The Rapide and Black Shadow had virtually the same internals, although early Shadows had the higher bottom gear ratio of 7.25:1 rather than 9.1:1 and this could be obtained on special order. The gearbox camplate was drilled for lightness on most Shadows to facilitate a more secure change

Above

The springboxes are set here behind the eccentric for solo use. For use with a sidecar, it is a simple matter to change the trail by rotating the eccentric to position the springboxes to the front of the spindle, shortening the trail from 3¼ in. to 2½ in. and strengthening the springs. The HRD tank transfer was used until 1949 on Series B and C machines. However, Philip Vincent learnt that HRD was being confused with Harley Davidson, particularly in America, so the 'Vincent' scroll came into being. Genuine gold leaf was used for the gold lines. A transfer of the figure Mercury was on the top of the tank and on the steering head lug

Right

With the machine on the rear stand, the rear section of the mudguard will swing up to allow the wheel to be removed. Even with a rack attached there is still sufficient clearance. The basic design of the rear frame and suspension system goes back to when motorcycles were still a twinkle in Philip Vincent's eye. The triangulated frame was extremely stable and rigid and was a good companion to the girdraulic front forks, with or without a sidecar. The pivot point, where the frame was attached to the engine plates, featured tapered roller bearings which were more capable of sustaining side pressures, and they virtually lasted for ever. The shaft to operate the twin rear brakes ran through the same casing. A larger racing tyre could not be fitted to the early Series B frames without it fouling the mudguard. Consequently, frames were now made ½ in. longer. The seat stay lugs were curved; straight lugs indicates an early, usually shorter, frame. The twin springboxes were not adjustable but heavier springs were available for sidecar work. The addition of the damper in the Series C certainly helped handling, although the problem of leakage has usually encouraged owners to use a more modern alternative unit

Above

It's either a visit from outer space or it's Glyn and Marian taking a night ride

Left

Over the years, like many owners, Glyn Baxter has made modifications to his twin to suit tastes and touring requirements. A Gardner 12 volt conversion box boosts the six volt Lucas dynamo. Wheels now take a 4.10 x 19 front tyre and a 120 x 18 rear. In spite of regular use, with the weather as it comes, the machine is kept in sparkling condition throughout the year. The Gordon Griffiths rear subframe gives a combination of the later Series D style rear suspension and the facility to take three luggage boxes. A Scott oiler drips oil on to the lower chain just before it goes on to the sprocket. The Series D centre stand is a useful addition, especially when the bike is fully loaded. Vokes air cleaners were a spare made available by the factory and were vitally necessary for good engine protection when travelling in many areas; these are a modern alternative. To counter the often-felt sponginess of the front brake, reinforcing supports are frequently welded on to the standard steel brake plate and cam bush. The brake plates used here are copies of the Black Lightening's. Formally made of Elektron, magnesium alloy, modern reproductions are of stronger aluminium alloy, which also has better corrosion resistence. A second bridging fitting has been attached on the outside of the balance beam to prevent any flexing at the balance beam pivot point. The original bridge plate was of ⅛ in. light alloy and the fitting of a heavier duty plate has the same effect and still looks standard

The timing side of the 998cc engine, with the steady plate not yet fitted, on this engine being rebuilt by Bob Dunn of Bolton. Early, and somewhat noisy, large idlers were of phosphor bronze and were soon replaced by a forged alloy component, so that it would expand with the alloy crankcase. The two cam gears, the breather valve pinion and the half-time pinion were of nickel chrome molybdenum steel. However, due to problems with the large idler sometimes failing and shedding teeth and the fact that it did not become as hot as other components anyway, the racing steel idler became available and proved to be a better option. It was often felt that the timing gear was excessively noisy, but this was not always the case – much depending on the quality of the rebuild. To some extent the noise of the all alloy engine was slightly magnified because of being attached to the oil tank. The valve lifting mechanism, to be fitted in the top left, opened the exhaust valves to assist kick-starting and to cut the engine at low revs. The automatic timing device was fitted with a fibre pinion rather than metal so that any play would have a less severe affect on the magneto. Unfortunately the pinion could wear and fail suddenly. For a rev-counter to be fitted, the ATD was replaced by a rev-counter drive dog and the magneto advance and retard was controlled manually

The Series C Black Shadow was very much the flag ship of the Vincent marque. With a top speed of 125 mph and an ability to reach 60 mph in first gear, acceleration was 0-60 in 6.5 seconds, or even less with the lower bottom gear. With a compression ratio was 7.3:1 and 1 ⅛ in. carbs, it delivered 55 bhp at 5700 rpm. Weight was 458 lbs, three pounds more than the Rapide. The power and performance of the Black Shadow was a new experience to most motorcyclists at the time. In 1952 there was a particular shortage of chrome and a number of machines were fitted with black wheel rims, as seen here on Terry Gee's machine

Above

The big Vincent represented a romance and glamour that was new to many people. Both in styling and performance, the bike was unlike anything people had experienced before and particularly in Europe after the hard war and post-war years, the machines had a special impact on the motorcycling public. It was to be many years before other manufacturers were able to match the Vincent's power and effortless performance

Right

The powerhouse of the Series C Black Shadow. The barrels were of the same light alloy used for the crankcases and were fitted with cast iron liners. Original pistons were Specialloid and the modest compression ratios of 6.8:1 on the Rapide and 7.3:1 on the Shadow gave a good combination of performance and flexibility. The normal pistons used today are Omega with closer clearances and better rings. As well as giving less piston slap and thus being quieter, when coupled with a sealed inlet valve there is a reduction in the amount of oil used. Original oil consumption for the twin was about a gallon per 1500 miles – a quantity which is not acceptable today. The cylinder heads used on the Series A were both the same, with the carb on the right. It was felt, erroneously, that this design was more efficient than with the carb on the left. Because this resulted in the front carb being virtually inaccessible, the front head was redesigned for the Series B. As both components were completely new castings, no proper explanation has ever been found as to why the twin now had two types of head – it was possibly purely for appearances sake. The heads were of a much stronger alloy than used on rest of the engine, and all heads were ported to take a 1⅛ in. carb. Any modern rebuild of the head will usually involve using valve seats made from sintered steel which are compatible with unleaded fuel. Very early timing covers had more pronounced oil channels cast in. During the change-over from the 'HRD' to the 'Vincent' logo in 1949, some crankcases and inspection caps had the 'HRD' ground off, as with these caps. Crankcases, barrels, heads and covers on the Shadow and the Lightning were given pyluminised anti-corrosion treatment prior to black stove enamelling

Above

To say the least, the crankcases on the Series B and C were strong. Sand-cast in alloy to aircraft specification they were extensively ribbed for added rigidity. The strength and design in this area were largely responsible for the lack of vibration in the machine. The crankcases were always made as a matched pair, with final machining completed on both halves together, with the same number being stamped on each half. Timing and chaincase covers were similarly matched and stamped, so fitting different covers would require additional machining to ensure a neat finish. This bike was built from bits by Andrew Walker

Right

Original tyres were 3.00 x 20 on the front and 3.50 x 19 on the rear. Being made of steel, the rims were chromed and painted black in the centre with a red line on both sides. Due to availability of tyre sizes, 19 in. and 18 in. wheels are normally used today. From the very early days of Vincent-HRD, when spokes were attached to the brake drums, separated spoke flanges were used, thus removing the stresses from the drums. With this facility, the brakes and the drums could be removed without disturbing the rest of the wheel. Various lumps of metal and bits of wire can be seen for balancing purposes, but lead weights fitted to their own rim holes were originally used. Shadows, racing models and the later Black Prince had ten bolts attaching the flanges and drums to the rear hubs, otherwise five bolts were used. The 'indestructible' Timken tapered roller bearings were fitted, as on the rear frame. Chromed pipes were standard and were attached by means of finned nuts screwed into the cylinder heads. With the passing of the years, stripped threads in the exhaust ports were not uncommon, to be remedied by rethreading or fitting an insert. Replacement stainless steels pipes have also been made. With all settings correct, pipes will retain their proper colour, but a weak fuel mixture and wrong ignition timing can produce bluing of the chrome and a dark straw colour on the stainless steel

Above

A talisman for the Black Shadow was the 5 in. 150 mph speedometer and owners frequently put one on other models because of its distinctiveness. The 100 mph mark is simply passed by

Left

Tony Summers bought this twin as a basket case from America and it was made up from three different machines. Engine internals are of Black Shadow specification. The engine number sequence for the Rapide started F10AB/1/ followed by the individual engine number. The Black Shadow had /1B/. A number of machines were ordered to Shadow spec with a polished engine and these were referred to as a White Shadow with the number identification of /1A/. The Black Lightning was coded /1C/. There were nine Series B and seventeen Series C White Shadows, with one model finished in red, although many owners have gone over to this specification privately

Above

Long distance touring was one of the principal functions the designers intended for the bikes. Series C and D twins are seen here in the north of England

Above left

Alan Wright's spare bike is an immaculate Shadow, which is kept safe and dry in the office

Left

The option of Chinese Red was available for export – 106 Rapides and 17 Comets were finished in this way and most of them went to America. The Touring Rapide featured steel valanced mudguards, higher handlebars and sealed beam light units for the States. Tyre sizes were 3.50 x 19 and 4.00 x 18. In 1951, Sid Biberman was helping the local Indian dealer unpack some Vincents from their cases and was so bowled over by the sight of the machine that he bought it on the spot. He has been heavily involved in Vincents ever since and runs a classic motorcycle restoration business in Norfolk, Virginia. His restored model shows the striking appearance of the Tourer. Apart from the 5 in. speedo and the rear light which should be red, the bike is quite standard (Photo Sid Biberman)

Above

A little extra glitter with the forks highly polished and golden colour of well used stainless steel pipes

Left

The busy workshop belonging to Terry Gee might be seen as grounds for divorce. Two bikes running and three more in different stages of completion

Right

Made between 1949 to 1954, in some ways the Series C Comet was the best bike made by Vincents. Although it lacked the speed and glamour of the twin, it was extremely solid, well built and reliable. Weighing 390lb and thus considerably lighter than the twin, handling was better, particularly at low speeds. The wheelbase of 55¼ in. was ¼ in. shorter than the twin because with the smaller gearbox the rear frame pivot point could be brought forward slightly. The Comet gave the impression it could run forever as an ideal work-horse, with minimal attention. In good order, it could reach 90 mph, cruise at 65-70 and return 75 mpg. The Vincent pioneered the dual seat and produced an attractive, comfortable and stylish example, originally made by Feridax. The base, which was reinforced by metal fittings, was plane, unpainted plywood, although painted waterproof ply is a more usual choice today. Seat height at the rear could be adjusted by turning the eyebolts. The tool tray was a slide fit under the saddle and was easily accessible. Standard mudguards were made of aluminium alloy, with steel reinforcing strips

Above

With the engine set at an angle of 25 degrees, the original compression ratio was 6.8:1 and the carb was the same as the Black Shadow's – 1⅛ inches. The bottom end of the Comet must be one of the most robust of any 500cc machine and is mainly responsible for the low level of vibration through the rev range. Both the five plate clutch and the gearbox were made by Burman and Sons Ltd, and were components used on many other motorcycles. Dick Perry restored this Comet as near as possible to the same condition as the machines left the factory. The engine and aluminium parts were not highly polished and most components were finished in cadmium plate rather than chrome. Dick even went to the trouble of using original machine washers with chamfered edges. The standard petrol tank held 3½ gallons, with a tyre pump fixed under the right side. The rear of the tank dipped in order to collect any dirt and grit

Above

A considerable number of components were the same as on the twin, including the oil and petrol tanks, front forks, rear frame, wheels, brakes, electrics, guards and controls. When Peter Elvidge restored his Comet, he kept it to a very standard set-up. The only non-standard items are the addition of coil ignition, stainless steel fittings and highly polished alloy. Most owners have moved away from the original rather drab appearance of the crankcases and covers. Peter's motorcycle has tended to win every concours event it has entered

Right

The inspection caps were easily removable to give access to the tappet adjuster. The rocker assembly was lubricated by the feedbolt which held it in place. The assembly was long lasting and potential wear in the rocker tunnel caused by movement of the rocker bush could be eliminated by the use of a modified lockable feedbolt, produced as a non-standard item. Upper valve guides of hiduminium and lower guides of aluminium bronze were fitted. The rocker operated on the valve stem collar situated between the two guides. With this layout, the valves remained accurately aligned, received less lateral pressure from the rockers and the overall height of the engine was reduced. Over the years, many modifications have been tried on engine parts, such as roller-bearings on the rockers and cam spindles. These, along with most others, have not proved worthwhile and the standard set-up has usually been reverted to. The push-rod tubes were made of stainless steel. Early cylinder heads had no pillar between the ribs in the middle, but this was added for extra strength. This example has an original type of suppressor cap. In total some 8,000 Series C machines were made

Above

Series A machines had a simple chain adjuster, but it required a spanner. The Series B and C machines had a more refined device. Once the wheel had been released by hand with the tommy bar, the chain could be adjusted, also by hand. The adjuster was spring loaded and was made of aluminium with a stainless steel sleeve. The wing nuts on the brake cams meant that each rear brake could be adjusted individually, also by hand. The rear sprocket on the Comet was fitted on the left side, as dictated by the requirements of the Burman gearbox. The standard sprocket had 48 teeth, while the twin had forty-six. It was a simple matter to change the sprocket to suit sporting events or touring. The rear brake drums could both be fitted with sprockets, so the wheel could be easily turned round to change the gearing. For strengthening purposes, the rear brake cam bushes were fitted with aluminium steady sleeves. The early Vincent HRD's started fitting stainless steel parts and this practice was extended in 1946. Brake rods, brake cable trunnions and motion blocks, tommy bars and battery strap were among the stainless steel parts fitted. Early post-war machines also featured such items as stainless steel kick-start crank and banjo bolts. Since then, there has been an ever increasing list of stainless steel parts made privately and available for the Vincent, such as front fork spindles and eccentrics, nuts, bolts, washers, springs, spring boxes, exhaust pipes, silencers, handlebars and mudguards

Right

The rear cylinder is replaced by an aluminium tie-bracket. This bracket also served as a fixing point for the footrests and the gearbox. Comet footrests did not fold up and lacked the styling of the twin's. In the event of the bike being dropped, the tie-bracket could easily be damaged. It is possible, however, to modify the hangers by welding on rear footrest pivots. With an engine shock absorber similar to the twin's, the primary chain was only a single chain, which was adjusted by moving the gearbox. The brake pedal lever was the same as the twin's

Above

The author's Comet was built for regular use, hence the addition of indicators, twin mirrors, fully enclosed rear chain, large horns on the crash bar and stainless steel spindles, nuts and bolts everywhere. When being used daily in the centre of London, although many people were pleased to actually see a Vincent on the road, it was surprising how many people thought it should not be used in this way on the grounds that it would get dirty in the rain or start to wear out. It was registered in July 1952 and numbered 9144. With a total of over 11,000 motorcycles built, it meant that over the following 2½ years only about 1,450 Series C machines were made

Right

The sheer weight of the twin has meant that very few women have ever used one. The Comet, however, is a more realistic proposition. Sue Barton rides her machine regularly, as well as around Europe to continental rallies. Restored by husband Dick with parts from several bikes, this was one occasion when there were not too many complaints about there being a cylinder head in the oven and an engine on the kitchen table. With the thinner seat lowered slightly, the height is more convenient for Sue, while the A10 handlebars provide her with a comfortable riding position. The bike features the 5 in. clock and Mk 1 Amal carb and quite a lot of stainless steel. Compression ratio has been lowered to just below 7:1 by means of a compression plate, and with the electronic ignition points the bike can literally be started first time by hand. Dick is in the background with his twin, which was registered in February, 1955, and is believed to be the last Series C Rapide made

Above

A personalised Comet with 13 in. wheels and a colour to make its presence known. The Comet still makes a suitable power unit for an outfit

Right

For those who feel the Comet has little glamour, Ian Lang's example defies that. It was bought in 1964, after spending three years of its life in a back garden. Ian has improved it over the years in between race meetings, sprints, rallies, trips abroad and journeys to work. He has remained loyal to the Comet and has never really been tempted to move on to a twin

Above

The standard rear sprocket for sidecar use was likely to be with 56 teeth, and the rear wheel had the facility of taking a sprocket on both sides, so it was a simple matter to turn the wheel around for a change of ratios. This outfit, belonging to Bernie Stovin, is fitted with standard wheels. The solo front tyre is fitted because Bernie finds it handles better than with the square profile tyre. The wheels, in fact, could be a weak point in the system. With continuous hard riding and fast cornering, the long spokes received considerable forces and it was not uncommon for spokes to brake and the wheel to collapse. To help avoid this, 16 in. rims were often fitted and as well as lowering the bike which improved stability, their extra strength paid dividends

Left

The top two sidecar fittings were bolted to the UFM and the lower two were bolted to the engine unit. The small triangulated rear frame and the girdraulic front forks were so strong that they were easily able to cope with the extra lateral forces placed on these components, which was certainly not the case with most other suspension systems. The eccentrics were turned to position the springboxes at the front, thus reducing the trail. At the same time, the front springs were almost vertical and so their effective strength was increased. Heavy duty springs were available for the rear springboxes and for heavy loads some riders would replace the damper with an extra springbox. The later concentric carbs, as fitted here, do not give the same surge problems on an outfit as the standard carbs with separate float chambers

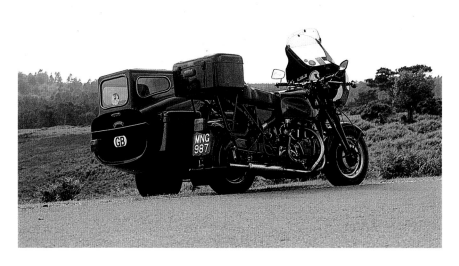

Above

There is still a market for various types of sidecars. Apart from their own fun value, they enable the family man to take the family and still use a motorcycle. Dave Johnson favours this child/adult sidecar, but in his case it is usually the dog that occupies the rear seat. This chair is the last of 25 made by Martello Plastics in 1989 and is in very strong glass-fibre. The wheels are 13 in. car wheels with radial tyres. Numerous custom tanks have been made over the years, with larger capacity, especially favoured by tourers

Right

The power and torque of the twin engine made it an ideal choice for sidecar enthusiasts. At the design stages, the specific requirements for sidecar use were borne in mind. The unit construction engine combined with the upper frame member was an extremely robust structure

Left

A touring outfit complete with touring mudguards and high wide sidecar handlebars. Two very rare features are the Vokes air filters, an optional extra during production, and the hydraulic sidecar brake. The slave unit can be seen fitted into the rear brake rod

Above

Ian Poskett really makes his Rapide earn its keep. Fitted with Steib sidecar and trailer and loaded with family and luggage, continental touring trips are a regular event for this set-up. A five gallon alloy tank has been fitted. Luggage equipment was essential for touring particularly on a solo machine and two panniers with special frames were an option from the factory.

The attractive cases were covered with hide, lined and featured quality fittings and a leather handle. They were attached on pegs and secured with straps. Being slung well forward under the passenger's seat they had minimal effect on handling, although longer pillion footrests were necessary. Not many were sold and they are an extremely rare item today. Vincent also made their own loop crash bars fitted to the front upper and lower sidecar mounting holes but most owners have never even seen them

Left

Black Shadow and Comet carbs and adaptors were 1⅛ in., made in bronze whereas the Rapide's were 1¹/₁₆ inches in alloy. Apart from the Shadow front carb, they were made of zinc aluminium alloy, finished in silver-grey paint. The Shadow front carb was not the normal mass-produced item and consequently was a special sand casting in brass finished in dull chrome. When polished a spare brass carb makes an attractive paper weight!

Above

Over the years, considerable effort has been expended to improve the Vincent's electrical system and lights. Early changes involved the fitting of the French Marchal and Cibie headlamp reflectors, which was a great improvement. Many owners have had Miller and Lucas dynamos rewound to 12 volts thus keeping the outside appearance of the machine standard. This helped, but a higher engine speed is required to generate a charge. Numerous systems of gears and flexible drives have been devised to utilise car dynamos and alternators, and even the fitting of alternators on to the primary chain case and driven by the ESA. In this photograph, the owner fitted a car generator in the seventies, while today a small Fiat unit can be driven directly from the standard dynamo drive. Very small and powerful alternators can now give the Vincent lights on a par with modern makes. One or two owners have installed electric starters from Japanese bikes. Positioned under the distributor cowling on the Series D, a chain drive is attached to the ESA

The Grey Flash started life as a Comet tuned by George and Cliff Brown in early 1949. The cylinder head ports were streamlined and polished. The inlet port and manifold were eventually enlarged to take a 32mm 10TT carb. Lever type petrol taps were fitted. The flywheel, conrod, rockers and cam followers were polished and normal compression ratio was 8:1. The magneto was a BTH TT. Numerous parts were drilled for lightness as well as the front forks being cut away inside and the final weight of a racing Grey Flash was 330 lb. On the works machine, the rear seat stays were modified for more effective suspension on road races and the rear frame damper lugs have been cut off. The large pushrod nuts used here were only on the works machines. With the gear change lever reversed in this way, it meant the gear positions were also reversed. The large gear indicator was fitted because the Albion box was difficult to change when cold, so a kick with the heel worked wonders for initial use.. One rear brake has been removed to save weight, with the sprocket fitted to an aluminium carrier. The bike rather missed the brake because the extra heat generated could burn the paint off the drum. The seat is a non-standard part but comes from the mid-fifties

Above

The Grey Flash was offered in three forms: as a racer, a road-going machine and as a roadster with racing accessories. This example was restored by Glyn Baxter and features a 1¹⁄₁₆ in. RN carb, 9.5:1 compression ratio, lightened and polished flywheel, lightened timing gear, Corrillo conrod and BSA B50 piston. Tyres are 19 front and 18 rear, rather than the original 21 and 20

Above right

Albion gearbox and clutch were used, providing a greater range of ratios, with a modified tie bracket being necessary for the Albion box. The alternative racing gear change was similar to the Black Lightning's

Right

The standard rear sprocket for general use had 48 teeth. This example has 56 teeth, more suitable for sprinting and short circuits. The main riders of works Flashes in the early fifties were George Brown, John Hodgkin and John Surtees, who was apprentice at Vincents at the time. With a top speed in excess of 110 mph, the Grey Flash had the potential to be very competitive at the top level with a sustained works challenge. In fact, a weak financial position meant that the factory did not do a great deal on the works-sponsored scene, but they did enter four machines in the 1950 Senior TT. Although their highest place was 12th with Ken Bills standing in for the unwell George Brown, it flew the flag and greatly improved the public's confidence in the company. This provided a good boost for sales for many months and their trading position changed so favourably that they were no longer under the control of the receiver

Above

The finish of the Grey Flash was attractive with the aluminium parts being anodised grey, grey stove enamel, dull chrome and the engine fine sand blasted to a matt finish. Glyn has maintained his Flash in racing trim and it still gets used on club circuits. Here he is braving a wet and greasy track

Right

This road-going Flash is one of only three ever made. Engine specification was similar to standard Grey Flash's with the addition of electrics from the Comet. They could be fitted with the Brooklands Can and it was found to be better for performance than the standard silencer. The racing dual seat is seen here, it being a slimmer version of the standard seat. Altogether, just 31 Grey Flashes were made over seven months in 1949 and 1950

The machine used by Rollie Free to set
his records led to the introduction of the
Black Lightning. Compression ratio was
to order ranging from 9:1 on petrol up to
around 13:1 on methanol. With 9:1 CR,
power was 70 bhp at 5600 rpm. High lift
Mk 2 cams, 32mm 10TT carbs and
Lucas KVF TT magneto were fitted.
The 2 in. straight-through exhaust pipes
gave a megaphone effect and produced
more power, while the pipe nuts had to
be turned down to clear the larger
diameter. There were alloy wheels and a
rev-counter. Conrods were of 85 tons/sq.
in. high-tensile steel and along with the
flywheels were polished. The large idler
was of steel and case hardened. There
was a 8000 rpm rev-counter rather than
a speedo. The gearbox had double
backlash on all gears and a lightened
cam plate and actuating arm, while a
change of gearbox sprockets was
available for different events. A higher
bottom gear was fitted to bring all four
gears closer together. Unnecessary items
such as lights, dynamo, kick-starter and
prop-stands were removed to save weight.
The magneto cowling was not required
because the KVF TT mag was
waterproof and its removal helped the
cooling of the oil filter. The usual
drilling for lightness was undertaken, but
the fork blades were never cut away, as
on the Grey Flash, for safety reasons.
The wheels of the chain-adjusters were
removed to save an almighty few ounces.
The standard big end gave extremely
good service for many events, but a
caged-roller big end was advisable for
sustained periods at high revs and later
bikes were fitted with this component.
Vincent were to regret not following
their own advice here, at Montlhery.
Other components were also replaced by
steel equivalents, such as the breather
pinion and the oil-pump worm. Due to
the absence of sufficient 1000cc races in
Britain, most interest in the Black
Lightning came from overseas.

Combustion chambers were fully polished and the inlet port streamlined to take the larger racing carbs. Four sizes of carbs were used over time – 1¹/₃₂ in. at first then 1¹/₁₆ inches. When it came to enlarging the inlet ports on the rear head, the port was very close to the rocker tunnel and there was a danger of breaking through the tunnel wall. Because of this, all but the first few Lightnings were fitted with two front heads, where this problem did not arise. Carb sizes could then be increased to 1¼ in. and 1³/₁₆ inches. In fact, the thickness of the rear head tunnel wall varied and in some cases considerable inlet port enlarging was quite possible. Valves were polished and the valve rockers were also polished and finished at equal weight. The clutch also received special attention. The clutch shoe carrier, plate carrier and engine sprocket were both lightened as on the Shadow, while the drum was modified by having larger slots to take a one-piece Ferodo fibre plate. The hole in the cover was to provide cooling. Since production ended, there has been a trend with some motorcyclists both on and off the track to change the standard clutch for an alternative multi-plate version. The reason given is usually to obtain a quicker change at high revs. Strange then that the factory bikes and well-prepared private machines had few problems here and were able to win races and break lap records, both solo and with sidecar, using the standard clutch, usually competing against multi-clutched machines

On the Lightning the brake plates were made of Elektron – magnesium alloy. They were stronger and much lighter than the steel plates. They also featured ribbed supports and air scoops with a gauze insert were screwed on. In addition, Oilite bushes were fitted into the cam bosses. One problem frequently experienced with the Black Lightning concerned the tyres. The main supplier of racing tyres at the time was Avon and they had been rather slack in developing new technology to cope with the power of the engine. Not too many riders could handle the lack of traction and nurse the power properly on to the track. As a result, they were not able to get the best out of the machine. About 24 Black Lightnings were made originally, but various attempts have been made to pass off replicas as the real thing. Consequently, careful authentication of newly discovered examples would be required

The Series D

The years 1954 and 1955 saw the production of six new Vincent models. The Series D machines had a number of modifications and were of innovative design, but they very much represented the swan-song for Vincent motorcycle production. During 1953, sales had been falling, the bikes had not changed for four years and the stimulus of new models was required. The earlier post-war boom in the sale of motorcycles had tailed off and new markets and higher profit margins were needed for these specialist bikes. The Vincent had certainly been proved to be fast and reliable and with the availability of improved grades of fuel and race-proved tuning, it would have been possible to produce an even higher performance machine. Instead, Philip Vincent preferred to concentrate on the touring and high-speed roadster qualities of the machines. To this end, full enclosures were designed and the result, first seen at the Earl's Court Show in autumn 1954, was a machine of unusual and streamlined appearance with good weather protection. The Black Knight was the enclosed version of the Rapide, the Black Prince that of the Black Shadow and the Victor was the enclosed Comet.

The Vincent became the first motorcycle with glass-fibre covers and the most powerful bike with full enclosures ever made. Immediate doubt was expressed about the machines stability in cross-winds, but in practice this never seemed to be the problem that many sceptics expected. There were problems with the quality of finish of the first enclosures, however, so the company went to Microplas Ltd who were experienced suppliers of sports car bodies. The change meant a four month delay and with potential sales being lost and motocycle production being only a few Series C bikes, Vincent decided to release the Series D in open form. Consequently, the Series D Rapide and Black Shadow came on the market. The enclosed models were not to every one's tastes but whereas they could be said to

The differences in appearance between the Black Knight and Prince were minimal – plain brake drums on the front, a 120 mph rather than 150 mph speedometer and different name transfers. The Knight had a battle-axe above the Vincent scroll, the Prince a Medieval helmet, while the only Victor produced had a steel gauntlet and the name 'Victor'. The lines were in genuine gold leaf and were in an attractive sweep along the length of the bike. The tanks on the enclosed models were finished in black stove enamel with no decorations at all. A 1951 Black Shadow cost £402; a Series D Shadow cost £355 while the Prince cost £378. Despite some reduction in production costs, even in 1955, the manufacture and fitting of all the enclosures could not have been profitable at a mere £23

have had distinctive styling, the open models were merely distinctive. The rear suspension had been modified with the supports for the rear of the seat being taken down to the rear frame pivot point. This provided a much more comfortable ride, particularly for the pillion, but it meant that the rear end was somewhat ugly when not enclosed by the covers as originally intended.

One of the most significant events in Vincent records took place in this period. In 1954, Robert Burns and Russell Wright in New Zealand, put large port heads from Vincents on a Black Lightning to go with the $1\frac{7}{16}$ in. carbs and 13:1 CR. Fitted with a streamlined sidecar, they broke the world record at 155.2 mph on a wet road. In July 1955, Wright took the world solo record at 185.15 mph and Burns the sidecar record at 163 mph. With these titles it meant that Britain held world land speed records on 2,3 and 4 wheels, as well as the world air and water records. Losing the

sidecar record to a factory-sponsored supercharged BMW, Vincents fitted Picador big-ends and flywheels, higher geared oil pump and 1½ in. carbs with 11 in. induction adaptors. With barely sufficient sponsorship, they took their fully streamlined and enclosed machine to Bonneville, USA. Against considerable logistical problems, Burns achieved the world's fastest speed of 176.42 mph for the mile. Wright achieved 198.3 mph on the solo and with more time to perfect the fuel mix, a few more miles per hour would have taken the absolute solo record as well. Even so, it was the fastest speed attained by an unsupercharged machine.

By the mid-fifties, there was substantial competition from mass-produced motorcycles, from cheap and fashionable scooters and from an expanding supply of smaller family saloons, which were appealing to the Vincent's potential customers. The Triumph Tiger 650 and the Gold Star were thirty per cent cheaper than the Vincents, while the BMW R69, Manx Norton and the Black Lightning all cost around £470. Even so, it should have been possible for Vincents to sell more than their relatively small production in the world market with the right approach, especially with the world-wide publicity from the Burns and Wright records and the numerous national records by other riders. Vincents had eventually bought some expensive machinery for increased volume production, but there was now little chance of this ever being used to capacity. With the enclosed models available from March 1955, sales never really took off and production ceased on the December 16 1955, with not one of the 'D' machines having made a profit. Vincents had always built for quality and longevity. They were not prepared to reduce quality in order to lower the price and seemed unable to get over the hurdle of increasing production in order to reduce unit costs. According to the sometimes inadequate company records, and including a few models being made later from spares, a total of 105 Black Knights, 120 Black Princes and one Victor were built. By this time, there were 160 Rapides, 145 Shadows and one Comet. The scarcity of the Series D machines means they have commanded a higher price in the classic bike market, even though they are not altogether the most popular models. According to the engine numbers there was a total of 11,134 post-war Vincents made.

Left

Once the seat had been tilted forward and rested on the tank, the lower attachment nuts were released and the rear cowling lifted up, to be propped in position. A tubular frame of three steel hoops were bonded into the panels to provide support for the cowling as well as mounting points for the rear footrests. Note combined damper and spring rear suspension. The rear light was Lucas; the unit on the enclosed model was different from that on the open model, to blend in with the rear cowling. Panniers had been designed by Vincents but they never went into production. The frame for the rear cowling was already provided with the necessary fixing points. Standardisation, finally, with same style front head on both cylinders. Monobloc carbs, without the previous separate float chamber: no leaks

Above

The dual seat, which looked somewhat ungainly on the open models, now appeared quite compatible with the rest of the machine on the Prince.. The rear cowling protected the riders from wind and dirt and with the softer ride, the enclosed models were more popular than the open models with the pillion passengers. Side panels were easily removed with three thumb screws. Tyres were 19 x 3½ in. on the front and 18 x 4 in. on the rear but there were no longer tommy bars for quick wheel changes. The electrics on the D Series, including the wirng loom and light fittings, were all converted to Lucas, and more reliable coil ignition was adopted. The coil was bolted to the left side of the crankcase, rather too conspicuous on the open models. The dynamo was a 60 watt Lucas unit

Above left

The Vincent Prince logo was adorned with a silver mediaeval helmet. The screen and hand shields were bolted on, and an average height person could just look over the top of the screen. Substantial body protection was given and with the leg shields, it was easy to maintain an upright riding position at high speed while still wearing conventional clothes. The leg shields were fitted over front loop crashbars attached to lower engine plates and the upper sidecar mounting point

Above right

An ideal fitting for the Prince and Knight was the black perspex screen and although it was a factory option at the time, none were actually sold. Sales of the component were never really pushed, however, because Vincents also had a good supply of standard clear screens. The handlebar cowling featured the speedo, Lucas switch, ammeter and transfer. By necessity, the air levers were mounted upside down

Right

The UFM was redesigned for the Series D to accommodate the new rear suspension unit and was rather a retrograde step. The Series C oil tank was extremely strong and robust whereas now it was replaced by a weaker unit, involving 1⅛ in. tubing, while the oil tank was moved to under the seat. It did allow a larger capacity fuel tank with four gallons but it was prone to flexing and occasionally the rear casting has been known to crack. As before, the front casting attached to the steering lug and the rear casting to the rear suspension unit

Left

The first Series D models were completely without any enclosures and the improved rear suspension was exposed in a way not originally intended for this range. Apart from the rear seat and suspension, at first sight, the open bikes appeared to be very similar to the Series C's. All Series D engine covers were black stove enamel, while the crankcases, cylinder heads and barrels remained unpainted. As previously, the Rapide had plain front brake drums, but all 'D' models featured one ribbed rear drum and a newly designed water excluder on the sprocket side. In 1954, the crankcases were die-cast rather than sand-cast. The resulting castings were thinner, lighter and had a better finish. At the same time, there was some strengthening in certain areas such as the gearbox camplate lug running the full width of the crankcase. In addition, the sand-cast cases were dirty at first and the grit in the metal worked its way out during the early life of the engine. The change to die-cast must have been expensive at a time when profits were low and planned production only small. It is sometimes claimed that the Series D crankcases were porous and that oil would seep into the gearbox. In fact, all crankcases were made of the same

alloy but with the die-casting there were many blow holes in the castings. These were filled with an aluminium filler and oil could seep here. Also the mating surfaces were thinner and did not always line up accurately. There were other teething problems with the crankcases, such as some of the openings for the pushrod tubes were not square with the tubes, and were too large, resulting in oil leaks. The luggage panniers seen here were not a Vincent accessory, but were made by Craven

Above

The Series D Black Shadow was the only Vincent with its name on the tank, put on as a transfer. The Lucas ammeter contained an ignition warning light but the Lucas switch was said not to be as reliable as the Miller unit it replaced. Both fitted into a large Lucas shell and light unit. The brake light switch was now attached to the front fork and operated by the balance beam and front brake rather than the rear brake

Above

The earlier twin springs and damper were replaced by a combined Armstrong hydraulic unit. The rear of the seat was supported by a sub-frame down to the rear frame pivot point providing a fully sprung seat and 6 in. of suspension travel. The rear wheel now moved completely independently of the seat which was not the case with the more conventional swinging arm system. The resulting configuration was to become the norm on most motorcycles in the 1980's. The seat support lugs were no longer required on the rear frame but there was an extra boss into which the rear cowling support could be placed when the cowling was raised. The five pint oil tank is under the seat on the right with the tool box on the left. The seat could hinge up from the rear. A spanner was now required for the chain adjusters but they did allow for finer adjustment. Varley batteries replaced the previous Exide and the fixing bolt was simpler in design. The rear brake cam arm was fitted pointing down in order to clear the covers on the enclosed models

Left

Built in December, 1955, this is the last Black Shadow made and was restored by Dave Hills. It was not sold and registered until October, 1956, and some enclosed models were not sold until 1957. The Series C breather on the front of the crankcase was changed to one on the inspection cap of the front inlet valve. The 'D' ESA was sturdier than its predecessor, containing 44 rather than 36 springs, a heavier end-plate and a tab washer to lock the nut. There were other improvements. The steel idler spindle was a one-piece unit; longer, single fork springs replaced the double spings; and there was a new twin-blade primary chain tensioner

Stuart Jenkinson uses his Prince in the manner Philip Vincent intended. He runs Bike and Sun Tours leading motorcyclists on touring holidays around Europe. He bought the machine new in 1955 and has covered more than 500,000 miles. The bike answers to the name of 'Vinnylonglegs' and has had three big ends, a new set of drive side main bearings, new gearbox bearings, new brakes twice but still runs on its original timing side main bearings and original wheel bearings. Stuart did not have a problem with cross winds on an enclosed model but found that head winds upset the handling because of the front fairing being fixed to the steering. To remedy this, he developed his own fairing. He removed the lower covers to improve cooling at low speeds in hot climates. A Citroën alternator and electronic ignition have been fitted. Stuart found the Series D tubular UFM flexed too much so he replaced it with the Series C unit which he finds provides better handling. The standard 'D' oil tank was retained while the UFM with its six pint capacity is used as a spare fuel tank. Two 6-volt batteries are fitted in series in the fairing, along with sockets for electric shaver and tape player. The extra discs on the brakes were cast, ground and shrunk on by Stuart for better cooling and stiffening, and he has never had any brake-fade not even with substantial braking down mountain passes. There is a temperature measuring gauge on each cylinder and he finds that temperature variation really depends mainly on wind direction. Front and rear suspensions are equipped with Gas Spax dampers. The use of the Vincent for such high mileage touring is reminiscent of the Tony Rose feat. In November 1951, Rose set out to cover 100,000 miles on a new Black Shadow, named 'Rumplecrankshaft', with its 5 in. speedo sealed by Smiths of Cricklewood. After the first 20,000 miles and with winter approaching, a sidecar was fitted and 90 mph was a regular speed. In the days before motorways, it is hard to imagine how he managed around 250 miles a day and still earn a living as a private detective. After less than 15 months, Tony Rose achieved his target and the engine was stripped down under press supervision. Wear throughout was found to be negligible and the longevity and reliability of the Vincent was clearly demonstrated

Other Projects and Racing

In most people's minds, the name Vincent is synonymous with classic high performance motorcycles, but many other engine and engineering projects were undertaken by the Vincent company. Non-motorcycle ventures started before the outbreak of the Second World War and continued for several years after the production of the last Series D. Numerous items like fuses for rockets and bombs, casings for mines, industrial parts, milling jigs and components for war machinery and aircraft were turned out in their thousands by the Vincent works after 1939. Specialist milling machines and lathes were installed to enable volume production and the meeting of Ministry of Supply requirements. Special development projects were undertaken and although many interesting and successful engines resulted, they mainly experienced a surprising lack of long-term production success.

Among the government projects were the designing of a marine engine to be used on an air-sea rescue life-boat and the Picador engine. The Picador was a modified Black Shadow engine designed to be used to power a target aeroplane for gunnery practice. The specification was ambitious, with the target plane being radio controlled and in the event of any sort of failure, parachutes, shock-absorbing cushions and flotation bags would come into play. The tuned engine produced 75 bhp at 5800 rpm and 180 mph and was designed to run flat-out continually. The project started around 1949 and lasted into the mid-fifties. Considerable modifications were necessary to overcome unique problems. To enable inverted flight, Jack Williams spent over two years developing a successful fuel injection system. A barometric aneroid control was required to keep the air/fuel ratio constant at different heights. The engine had to be started by electric starter while the plane was on its launch ramp and the initial propulsion rockets were automatically ignited. A strengthened bottom end and a modified lubrication system with two-start driving worm on the oil pump were necessary to enable the engine to run at such continuous high performance while one of the biggest headaches was outside Vincent's jurisdiction. The aeroplanes were radio-controlled and not too successfully. The plane itself, called the U120D, was of a design which had little inherent stability and so required constant, highly skilful manoeuvring. Often this was not the case and certainly could not be possible once the plane flew into the clouds. After too many mishaps, the project was cancelled with about thirty engines having been made. The contract was certainly profitable for the factory but it did not develop into

Philip Vincent had already patented an engine which appeared would be suitable for marine use. Having left the Vincent company in 1937 to work for Velocette and AJS, Phil Irving rejoined the firm in 1943 to develop this engine to Ministry specification. It was required to power a self-contained 30 foot lifeboat to rescue pilots from a ditched aeroplane or which might be dropped by parachute from the bomb bay of a Shackleton. The engine was a 15 bhp 500cc two-stroke with two crankshafts. There were three cylinders and six pistons, with the centre cylinder charging the two outer working cylinders. They were ported together and with the two crankshafts, the port timings could be adjusted independently by changing the angle of the crankshaft for optimum performance and fuel consumption. Each crankshaft had four main bearings. It had a triple pump for oil, water and bilge and there was an Amal marine carburettor. The engine also had to be unfreezable and able to sustain an impact of 5G. In sea trials in a boat made by Uffa Fox and with the propeller restricted to 1430 rpm, the boat travelled 1,026 miles on 50 gallons and was well within the Ministry's specification. The casing was given an anodised protective coating against the sea water. Reverse gear and electric starter were also developed for the engine but after various delays, following the five prototypes, only 55 engines were ordered in the early fifties

the substantial order for Picadors that had been expected, otherwise the production life of the motorcycles might have been greatly extended. The men from the Ministry also demanded complete devotion to their cause and it meant that there was little testing-time available for motorcycle development. The bikes did not benefit much from the project and for some reason not even the fuel injection system was used further. This would have put the Vincent very much ahead of its time and would have been particularly effective on the outfits to overcome fuel surging caused by centrifugal forces.

The post-war years had seen a boom in motorcycle sales, but Philip Vincent felt this would fall away before long. As a result, he was keen to broaden the product base of the factory. The development of products for the government and industry were a move in this direction. Several varieties of industrial two-strokes engines were developed from the mid-fifties for use as lawnmowers, cultivators and pumps and as a result of this production, by the time the Vincent Company folded it had produced more two-stroke than four-stroke engines.

Using some of the information gathered by installing twin engines into Cooper cars, Vincents built a three-wheeled car for the twin engine. With the two wheels at the front and the single wheel with the Vincent rear frame at the rear it was very stable. The prototype featured an aluminium body, an independent front axle, rack and pinion steering and hydraulic brakes. At one stage, the Gunga Din Lightning engine was installed in the machine and it was raced on the track. Although tests were promising,

Vincents started making industrial engines in the fifties and they took on an increasingly more important role in the factory's production. One such item from the period is this lawnmower, known as the Rapier, with its 73cc two-stroke motor. Vincents made their own magnetos and even some coils until they started buying them in from Wipac. Easy to start and use, and with adjustable height, as a mower it was very efficient and quieter than many modern machines. A variety of industrial engines was produced in this period. One 75cc model would use petrol from the small tank for starting and once warmed up, it would be switched over to run on paraffin. Made of aluminium, it had a cast iron liner. The 99cc engine had an output of 4 bhp at 4500 rpm and was frequently used as a compressor, as a grain elevator engine or as an inboard engine on a dinghy. Two engines were combined to make a 200cc version and a 200cc single cylinder prototype was made. A pair of 100cc motors was even fitted to the front wheels of go-karts in the sixties by the Harper Group which took over the Vincent company, although only a few were sold

financial troubles prevented the continuation of this scheme.

After the Burns and Wright successes, the factory began preparations for their own world speed record attempts. Working on the test-bed and dynamometer at night, Johnny Penn and Ted Davis developed a blown engine to 119 bhp. Negotiations were underway to obtain sponsorship from Mogul Oil and a streamlined shell was being designed by Cambridge University. The overall height would have been about one foot lower than the Burns and Wright machine and the target figures were 250 mph solo and 200 mph with sidecar. One night, Johnny Penn set out alone for a reckless rough water sea-ride on an Amanda and was drowned. The project was put aside for a while and never completed. In due course, the machine was sent to Penn's brother in Australia.

The Firefly cyclemotor was built and sold from 1953 in an effort to supplement the flagging sales of the larger bikes. Around the same time, Vincents started distributing the NSU machines from Germany. The Quickly was a complete 50cc moped and Vincent distributed them for about a year, selling 1,000 machines a month. At nearly £60, the Quickly was almost the most expensive cyclemotor on the market and compared with the £38 for the Firefly. However, it proved to be a better and more reliable machine than the Firefly and the situation arose that the Quicklys were sold to dealers on condition they also took the Fireflys. With the Quickly, Vincents had an agreement to provide cycle parts for the NSU motorcycle engines. By containing 51 per cent British parts, the bikes could circumvent the Commonwealth Preferential Tariff arrangement.

The Versatiller was a versatile cultivator with the 75cc engine and is fitted here with a potato ridger. There were twelve attachments in all, including a hedge trimmer on a flexible drive, a circular saw and a digger for planting trees. Tools were kept in the box on the column. Of the three versions produced, the Mk 3 had a kick-starter

There were four models from 100cc to 250cc known as the NSU-Vincent Foxes, but they were nowhere nearly as popular as the Quickly. In 1954, after Vincents had established the market, the importers of NSU set up their own distribution company and Vincents lost the lucrative sales and servicing business of the Quickly. Vincents carried on producing the Foxes until September, 1955.

Over the years, therefore, the Vincent company embarked on numerous projects outside the field of the standard Vincent bikes. Little in the way of feasibility and viability studies were undertaken but they seemed to be vague 'shots-in-the-dark' in the hope that something would work out. In the late forties and again for a while in the early fifties, the factory could not meet the demand for the Rapide and Black Shadow. Nothing effective was done to substantially increase production to meet this demand or to reduce unit production costs and increase profitability. With more than 300 staff in the mid-fifties there was substantial overmanning in some departments and a considerable amount of pilfering. There was said to have often been a bad atmosphere within the company in the later years. The Vincent company undoubtedly had outstandingly creative engineers and designers throughout its life, as well as all the necessary technical skills to put their ideas into practice. Unfortunately, there were not other company members with sufficient managerial, financial and marketing abilities to fully exploit this expertise and take an overall view of the direction of the company.

The end for the Vincent company came with the production of the Amanda water scooter. This clever idea and good design again shows the visionary nature of some of Philip Vincent's concepts. Originally, such designs as the rear suspension, the central backbone oil tank and the enclosed models were all severely criticised at their introduction. Time showed the value of these features and the popularity of similar water scooters can be seen today. Unfortunately, the project was spoilt by inadequate quality control, a slack financial procedure and a rather unscrupulous distributor.

In the early seventies, Philip Vincent designed a one stroke engine with an oscillating ceramic piston. A prototype was made and the 125cc's produced a power output so enormous that like previous designs it became another Vincent development which outsiders viewed sceptically. Philip died in 1979, aged 71.

Above

Perhaps the best known of the lesser Vincent products is the Firefly – a cyclemotor produced from 1953. Millers, the makers of electrical components, had designed a 48cc two-stroke engine suitable for a bicycle and Vincents put this into production. Cyclemotors were becoming extremely popular at the time for reasons of convenience and economy. At first, the engine and attachments were sold as a kit, then later as a complete bike, and finally as a kit again until 1958. Jan Ragg is here riding her Firefly which is a 1953 engine in a 1958 frame, complete with generator/battery lighting system. It could just about reach 20 mph and cover 60 miles from ½ gallon tank. A popular frame at the time was the Philips with the sprung Webb forks

Left

The engine had a cast iron barrel, a detachable alloy head and a decompressor valve. Early Fireflys had a transfer on the cover rather than the embossed name. The position of the engine on the frame gave it a low centre of gravity and made it easy to ride. Problems arose early on, however. The roller was engaged on to the specially ribbed rear tyre to give propulsion, but the bonding used to attach the rubber roller on to its shaft was inadequate and the rollers were soon working loose. This problem was remedied by making the drive wheel a casting. The bike was felt to be temperamental, however, and prone to punctures because of the extra pressures on the tyre and a poor reputation quickly developed. About 3,000 Fireflys were made, although they were soon eclipsed by the NSU Quickly

The Amanda water scooter was to bring about the final demise of the Vincent company. Fitted with the industrial engine, this scooter had a promising beginning. It was well received by the public and when powered by the 200cc engine it could reach a speed of 20 knots. There was a cord-starter, an automatic clutch and the exhaust was directed into the water, while the propeller turned at engine speed. This machine is owned by Bob Culver and is seen here being ridden by Bryan Phillips, President of the Vincent Owners Club. Bob takes the Amanda occasionally to rallies and it tends to be the star of the show. The scooter has proved to be safe for a child to use and stable enough to carry a 19 stone man. A number found their way on to boating lakes and the machine had the potential for further tuning for more sporting use. The quoted power rating was 2.5 hp but the company was told to call it 25 hp in the States or the machine would never be taken seriously. Two Amanda engines successfully completed 1000-hour tests at full throttle and under full load. In 1956, the company received an order for 6,000 Amandas for America. Factory facilities were found in Wales and production began in earnest. With a nation-wide news feature on the Amanda in America and a large order, the future for the scooter looked assured. The shell was made of glass fibre, as on the Series D, but the supplier of the resin had kept his price to a minimum and then supplied an inferior and unsuitable product. Lack of quality control meant the resulting bodies were substandard and when some early machines were demonstrated in the States in front of the press, a combination of the sun and the engine heat severely weakened the tensile strength of the glass fibre, causing the shell to melt and collapse. The American distributor was a flamboyant character with a dubious track record and had been granted three months credit which was extended a further three months. With hundreds of scooters already shipped and more on the way, following the disastrous demonstration the order was concealed and no money received. Such events dealt a mortal blow to the already shaky Vincent company and in 1958 the bankrupt firm was sold to the Harper Engineering Co. Philip Vincent sold his share in the company in January 1960

In 1959, Vincent Engineers (Stevenage) Ltd became known as Harper Engines Ltd and was sold to Cope Allman in the sixties. In 1975, the Vincent part was sold to the Velocette Motorcycle Co. and following the cessation of spares production, in July, 1975, the VOC Spares Company was formed by the Vincent Owners Club. The Club, which itself was founded in 1948, became the main shareholder, with more than 51 per cent of the shares, and there were about 800 other shareholders, mainly club members and Vincent owners buying a few shares each. The purpose of the company is to continue the supply of as many Vincent components as possible and now there is a 93 per cent availability of parts and some 1500 different items are in stock. Many parts are periodically produced in batches and the company holds some of the original moulds. A considerable amount of restoration work still goes on, both on existing machines being rebuilt and on old bikes being discovered. Wrecks are still re-appearing from the hundreds that had been sold in Argentina. They are often in a very bad state – many repairs having been undertaken in the past with hammer, chisel and a bag of nails. Sales for the spares company are literally world-wide, including such areas as Europe, North and South America, Japan, Australia and Papa New Guinea. The company is located in a 1760 building by the canal in Lymm, Cheshire. Don Watson, who was Managing Director for nearly ten years, is seen here in the stores

Considering the number of records George Brown broke with this machine, much of Nero looks surprisingly like a standard Vincent. After the Second World War, George was special bike tester and racer for the factory, while both he and brother Cliff were working in the development department. With Gunga Din and the Comet Special, George Brown took many lap records. George's skill on the track could be seen by how he broke the lap record in the Clubmans TT at his first attempt. George Brown left the works in 1951 and he set up his own shop in Stevenage. Around this time, George had turned down the offer of a works ride for Norton — an offer that John Surtees, after gaining valuable race experience at Vincents and being part of the Montlhery team, eagerly picked up and so began his international career. A couple of bad crashes had persuaded George to give up road racing and concentrate on sprinting and hill climbs. Buying a burnt-out wreck for £5, a Rapide which ended up in the top deck of a London bus, the Browns built Nero and it experienced immediate success in 1953 on tracks like Brighton, Pendine Sands and Shelsley Walsh. Cliff left Vincents in 1954 to join George full-time and concentrate on the shop and Nero. The set-up of the bike was continually being changed and improved, with the engine lowered and with longer swinging arm for the sprints. It is seen here in road trim with AJS Porcupine front forks and wheel and home-made rear frame. In 1958 at Brighton, George and Nero covered the standing kilometre in 19.29 seconds averaging 117 mph and a terminal speed of 186 mph and so he became the fastest man on two or four wheels

Super Nero was built in 1962 and in due course there were two versions – 1000cc and 1148cc with a low rigid rear frame and 70cc Honda front forks and brake. At Duxford in 1964, George did the standing quarter mile in a mean time of 10.283 seconds and broke the world standing kilometre record at 19.48 seconds. Streamlined, with and without sidecar, the various machines broke numerous national and world records over the next few years such as the sidecar standing quarter mile in 11.806 seconds and 76,229 mph in 1966 along with four other national and three world records. The Browns also found time to prepare world record breaking 250cc Ariels and Royal Enfields. An important element in their continuous success was the reliability of the machines, and their preparation was such that any sort of mechanical failure was rare. With his 55th birthday approaching, it would have meant George would no longer be eligible for international record attempts. Just prior to this date, at Greenham Common, he took numerous records such as the flying-start kilometre with sidecar in 14.939 seconds

and an average speed of 149.732 mph. Due to the FIM age regulations, George was making British records higher than world records as the latter were not recognised. After a persistent campaign and managing to get the regulations changed, George achieved the flying kilometre in a mean time of 12.285 seconds at 182 mph in 1970. Also riding Super Nero with the sidecar, son Anthony became the youngest world record holder at the age of 20 with a time of 11.746 for the standing quarter mile in 1967. Tony is seen here holding Super Nero. One limiting factor at the time was the tyre technology and today the same machinery would doubtless return much faster times. George had reached a terminal speed of 236 mph and it had always been his ambition to go for the world speed record. Surprisingly, all his record attempts were largely self-financed and although sponsors provided components, he was never able to secure the backing to make the necessary trip to Bonneville, USA Ill health brought his sprinting career to an end and George Brown died in 1979, aged 67

The 2 in. SU carburettor on Super Nero with the Shorricks supercharger. Fuel was nitro-methanol and compression ratio about 8:1. With the Picador style flywheels, larger main bearings and Stellite cams and followers, power was around 125 bhp. The Vincent gearbox was driven by a multi-plate clutch. No oil circulation system was used to the heads, instead the valves and rockers were given individual squirts of oil prior to each run. Oil for the blower was contained in one of the frame down-tubes

The Mighty Mouse is another machine with a special place in Vincent and British motorcycling history. Over a number of years, a Comet engine was progressively tuned by Brian Chapman for drag racing. In its final form the 500cc was fitted with a Marshall supercharger and a 1¼ in. SU carb. The flywheel was standard but with a large Alpha crankpin, Weslake speedway steel conrod, Cosworth F1 piston and Norton Commando valve springs. The engine ran on a nitro/methanol mix with a 7:1 CR. The cam was at first hand-made then duplicated in Stellite and the alloy large idler had thinner timing gears. There were two Lucas SR1 magnetos and two plugs. The oil tank was where the magneto would normally be while the mags were driven from the dynamo position. There were three gears in a Norton box. In the 1977-8 season, Brian achieved an incredible 8.81 seconds and 157 mph for the ¼ mile, this with an 500cc engine designed in the forties. He was also the ACU drag champion

Above

A tooth belt drive was fitted rather than the more usual V-belt of the time. The fact that Mighty Mouse was so light and low was extremely beneficial and the machine was always particularly good at the starts. This was the first sprint bike in Britain to be fitted with a wheelie-bar, at Silverstone in 1974, much to the amusement of the other competitors, until the improved results proved its value. The Mighty Mouse was superseded by Super Mouse, featuring a twin engine with two superchargers, an overdrive unit gearbox and slider clutch. Brian's best time was 8.25 seconds and 170 mph for the ¼ mile, and made it the fastest British single engine bike

Right

In the early seventies, Ron Vane completed the building of a sprint machine, known as 'The Thing'. With the twin rear wheels being less than 8 in. apart, it qualified as a three wheeled cyclecar. 135 lbs of ballast had to be carried in lieu of a passenger which brought overall weight up to about 650 lbs, with a length of twelve feet. The 998cc engine ran on methanol with 12.5:1 CR, 32mm 10TT9 carbs, oversize inlet valves, Norton gearbox and hydraulic clutch with 600 pounds spring pressure. There was a tubular chassis, aluminium body and glass-fibre nose cone. No suspension was fitted in order to improve steering and traction. In the autumn of 1972, Ron broke six national and five world records. Among the records there was the standing start quarter mile at 13.925 secs and 64.73 mph, the flying start quarter mile at 6.945 secs and 129.58 mph and the flying start kilometre at 17.695 secs and 126.41 mph. The original machine no longer exists and this is

the Mk 2 version. The engine was fitted with a Rayjay turbo in the mid-seventies at a time when this modification was quite rare. Again CR was 12.5:1, but with a 2 in. S & S full flow super fuel carb. The methanol was forced through under variable boost pressure. There was also an optional nitrous oxide injection system which could be used at full throttle. Pressure relief valves were fitted in the event of back firing to protect the turbo. There were two plugs per cylinder and electronic ignition. A two speed Bewley gearbox was combined with a three plate 9 in. slipper clutch which automatically cut in at 3500/4000 rpm once the engine was in gear. With the brakes applied, boost pressure was increased before take-off. Early power tests showed 104 bhp at 4000 rpm and 170 bhp at 7000 rpm, when the mainshaft broke, so detuning was necessary. Developments included stronger flywheels, mainshafts and front axle, resiting the turbo to get equal exhaust pipe lengths and the fitting of a torque converter prior

to the slipper clutch. This necessitated the fitting of an electric starter, powered by an auxiliary battery, as the rear wheels were disengaged from the engine, whereas previously the vehicle was push-started in gear. Eventually Ron considered that the fuel-enriching devices had become too complicated and the vehicle was too heavy to be truly competitive. Major changes would have been required and business commitments meant the project was not pursued after the mid eighties

Above

A beast at rest. John Renwick's outfit is a regular competitor at vintage meetings around Britain. John claims it is the most powerful petrol- powered Vincent in the world, generating 100.5 bhp at 6350 rpm. Running on 100 octane av-gas through 1 ⅛ in. GP carbs with home-made cams and crank, development work is undertaken with regular testing on a dynamometer. This is essential when experimenting with cam profiles and timings and for checking reliability. John's front brake incorporates two cams each side and although not of original design it does at least use standard components. The front end is modified and so is the position of the eccentrics

Right

Rowland Mettam and Peter Cascoyne take a bend on their very smart outfit during a classic race

Vincent engines have found there way into racing cars in the past. The regulations for Formula 3 car racing from 1946 and through the fifties were for 500cc capacity. As there were no car engines of 500cc made, the competitors turned to motorcycle engines and among the first was the car built by Colin Strang and Neil Shorrock using a Series A TT Replica engine. Used for hill climbs, it ran on methanol and produced 46 bhp. John Cooper was making the most successful cars for this category with his pioneering use of tubular frames and magnesium alloys. This car is owned and raced by Dennis Price. It is a Cooper Mk 8 and was the first with a completely tubular frame and alloy wheels. The body is aluminium and there is independent suspension with transfer leaf springs. The car was designed for a vee-twin so the stronger chassis is 2 in. longer than the 500cc version with the engine bay being made 4 in. bigger by shortening the cockpit. Dennis also has a twin engine for the same machine. Drive is by chain through a Norton gearbox and the hand gearchange can be seen on the right. Twin engines and Black Lightnings were put in a Cooper chassis and a car driven by Eric Winterbottom was clocked at 132 mph. Winterbottom also bought two unique Vincents, known and 'half-thousands'. They were 1000cc crankcases with the rear cylinder blanked off thus making the engine capacity 500cc, but being unit construction, the Vincent gearbox was retained. Rapid engine changes meant participation in two classes in one day! When back in Australia, Phil Irving prepared and maintained a supercharged Lightning in a Mk 4 chassis. Bored out to 1130cc and raced by Lex Davison, the team was virtually unbeatable on hill climbs, winning the Australian Hill Climb Championship three times in the mid-fifties

Left

Dennis Price's Comet/Cooper engine during its rebuild by Bob Dunn. The timing gears and steady plate have been considerably lightened. The magneto drive is ready for a rev-counter, while the dynamo opening has been blanked off. The engine has a 2 in. inlet valve, a 1⅛ in. Del'Orto twin float carb and a 2 in. exhaust port. With a CR of 13.5:1 it runs on methanol, while a Mk 2 cam and Corrillo conrod are fitted. There are two plugs and Interspan ignition. Vincents were not averse to selling just an engine and made 43 special engines for private projects such as this

Above

Starting in the mid-fifties there were numerous modifications made to Vincents in an attempt to bring them more up to date. Many were poorly conceived and executed and in due course there was usually a reversion to the more standard set-up. One of the more significant experiments was to put the Vincent engine into a Norton Featherbed frame, creating the Norvin. Peter Darvill put 'Lightnized' twin engines and singles into Norton cycle parts and it was based on these that motorcycle dealer, Tom Somerton, was making them to order. They were known as the Viscount and this is one of the six or seven he completed using the racing frame. The engine was a tight fit and many of the conversions were done by people with more enthusiasm than skill or common sense and they cut off a main lug on the rear of the crackcase. As well as being completely unnecessary, it meant the engine could not be converted back into the original Vincent rear frame. Fortunately modern welding techniques make it possible to repair this damage. Such conversions are less common today, however. With the Vincent being designed in the forties and well and truly 'classic', there seems to be little point in trying to pretend it can be modified to compete directly with modern machinery

Above

This Somerton example was bought as a worn-out wreck by Peter Carpenter and had been registered as a new bike in 1960. The engine is a very early Rapide, number 263 from 1947. The tank and seat are from the Dominator. Electronic ignition and Fiat dynamo have been fitted and total weight is 400 lb. Originally the engines had Mk 2 cams, wider rocker bearings with needle rollers, steel idler pinion, twin-start oil pump, full gas- flowed heads and 9:1 CR, although this has now been reduced to a more manageable 7.3:1 with low expansion pistons

Above right

In the mid-sixties, Fritz Egli in Switzerland, put the Vincent engine in his own cycle parts for sprints and hill climbs. After proving to be successful, he offered complete bikes or kits for sale. Ray Elger had achieved very fast times on his Brampton forked twin, with a best time of 12.18 seconds for the standing ¼ mile in 1966 at Santa Pod. After meeting Fritz Egli, he bought some of Fritz's cycle parts to make one of the first road-going Egli's in Britain in late 1968. The forks are Metal Profile with Norton front wheel and brake. A Lyta alloy tank was fitted

after the fibre-glass tanks were banned for sprinting. There are Norton rear shock-absorbers and home-made stainless steel silencers. The Specialloid pistons give a compression ratio of 9.6:1 and there are 36mm carbs and Mk 2 cams. Ray used a Lucas KVF TT magneto for racing but now ignition is electronic. The eight plate Norton clutch is in a Norton drum, modified to fit the Vincent clutch centre. All the gears have double backlash for quicker changes. Ray Elger covered the standing quarter mile in 11.9 seconds and reached 101 mph in 6.99 seconds and 220 yards. His standing kilometre time was 23.1 seconds and 132 mph at Duxford in 1970

Right

Also seen here is the 500cc Norvin built by Ray's son, Alan. A Comet engine in a Norton frame is an unusual combination. Alan Elger's bike has a wide-line featherbed frame and features numerous stainless steel parts made by Alan. There is a Norton twin leading shoe front brake, Manx central oil tank, ES 2 gearbox and a 40 amp alternator, driven by belt. The petrol tank is Dominator so the bike has been called a Com-Dom. The engine has 9:1 CR, a Mk 2 cam and 32mm Amal carb

With sponsorship from Castrol, Vincents set off for Montlhery in France in May, 1952 to attempt the '100 mph in 24 hour' record. They took four Black Shadows and three Black Lightnings, including Gunga Din. The Shadows had 8:1 CR, high lift cams, 1⅟₃₂ in. Amal carbs, special five gallon tank and 2 in. open pipes. There were nine riders in the team. The Montlhery circuit was 3.8 miles long with three straights and three banked sections at an angle of about 40 degrees and some 90 feet high. For timing purposes the rider needed to keep along the yellow line but sight of this line could be lost in the sun and then the rider had to make an instant judgement. To be below the line on the banking meant he would not have a good sweep coming into the straight and if too high above the line he was in danger of going over the unguarded top edge to almost certain death. The main problems arose because of the extremely hot weather conditions, made worse by the heat being trapped in the bowl area, giving a temperature of over 100° F. Rather than use the race-proved caged roller big-end, against advice, Philip Vincent was keen to use the standard big-end which in fact could not take the high revs and temperature. Also, Castrol wanted standard oil used (rather than racing 'R') which broke down in these conditions. Major problems were also caused by the tyres, because these were the most extreme conditions that motorcycle tyres had ever been subjected to. With the weight of a full tank, the rider and the bike travelling at speeds of 150 mph as it hit the banking, the Avon tyre expert reckoned there was a loading of about four tons on the rear tyre. This, together with the heat, meant tyres lasted only about 50 minutes, and even the use of the experimental slick tyres was to no avail. With Ted Davis trying for the 1-4 hour records at speeds of around 150 mph, the Avon man was watching through binoculars and saw the tyre was down to the canvas. With just seven minutes to go for the hour record, the attempt had to be stopped. Even so, at reduced speeds the team took eight world endurance records including the 11 hour record at 92.5 mph, that being achieved with Cyril Julian pushing the bike the last mile because of big-end seizure. Although there were not the successes the factory was hoping for, there was nevertheless considerable publicity and sales increased after the event. In fact, peak production was in 1952. Years later, Ted spent some time tracking down a Black Shadow used on that occasion. Eventually he found it in bits but almost complete in the possession of the Queen's cabinet maker at Sandringham. The lower front fork bracket was chromed and the top bracket was polished in order to see if any cracks appeared, although none did. A small plastic screen was fitted for the record attempts and, due to overheating problems, the front mudguards were removed to improve cooling

Specifications

Production dates

Series A
Meteor	1934 – 1939
Comet	1934 – 1939
Comet Special	1935 – 1939
TT Replica	1935 – 1939
Rapide	1937 – 1939

Series B
Rapide	1946 – 1950
Black Shadow	1948 – 1950
Meteor	1949 – 1950

Series C
Rapide	1949 – 1954
Black Shadow	1949 – 1954
Black Lightning	1949 – 1954
Comet	1949 – 1954
Grey Flash	1949 – 1950

Series D
Rapide	1955 – 1955
Black Shadow	1955 – 1955
Comet	1955 – 1955
Black Knight	1955 – 1955
Black Prince	1955 – 1955
Victor	1955 – 1955

Series A

	Meteor	Comet	Comet Special	TT Replica	Rapide
Capacity	499cc	499cc	499cc	499cc	998cc
Bore x stroke	84 x 90mm All models				
Compression ratio	6.8:1	7.3:1	8:1	8:1	6.8:1
Bhp & rpm	25 @ 5300	26 @ 5600	28 @ 5600	34 @ 5800	45 @ 5500
Ignition	BTH mag-generator or Miller dyno-mag			BTH TT mag.	Lucas MNV1 47'
Petrol tank	3¼ gals	3¼ gal	3¼ gal	5 gal	3 1/2 gal
Oil tank	3½ pints	3½ pints	3½ pints	8 pints	4 pints
Max speed	80 mph	90 mph	92 mph	110 mph	115 mph
Weight	385 lb.	385 lb.	385 lb.	335 lb.	430 lb.
Wheelbase	55 in.	55 in.	55 in.	55 in.	56 in.
Tyres	Front – 3.00 x 20 Rear – 3.25 x 19				
Carburettor	Amal 1¹⁄₁₆	1⅛	10TT 1³⁄₃₂	10TT 1³⁄₃₂	1¹⁄₁₆

Series B & C

	Meteor	Comet	Rapide	Black Shadow	Grey Flash	Black Lightning
Capacity	499cc	499cc	998cc	998cc	499cc	988cc
Bore x stroke	84 x 90mm All models					
Compression ratio	6.45:1	6.8:1	6.45:1	7.3:1	8:1	9:1 petrol
Bhp & rpm	26 @ 5300	28 @ 5800	45 @ 5300	55 @5700	35 @ 6200	70 @ 5600
Ignition	Lucas KIF GM2	Lucas KIF GM2	Lucas KVF GM1	Lucas LT KVF GM1	BTH TT magneto	Lucas KVF TT
Petrol tank	3½ gallons				3⅜ gallons	
Oil tank	6 pints all models					
Max speed	80 mph	90 mph	110 mph	125 mph	110 mph	150 mph
Weight	386 lb.	390 lb.	455 lb.	458 lb.	330 lb.	330 lb.
Wheelbase	55¾ in.	55¾ in.	56½ in.	56½ in.		
Tyres	Front – 3.00 x 20 Rear – 3.50 x 19					
Touring model, Comet & Rapide	Front – 3.50 x 19 Rear – 4.00 x 18					
Carburettor	1¹⁄₁₆	1⅛	1¹⁄₁₆	1⅛	10TT9 32mm	10TT9 32mm

Series D

	Rapide	Black Knight	Black Shadow	Black Prince
Capacity	998cc All models			
Bore x stroke	84 x 90mm All models			
Compression ratio	6.45:1	6.45:1	7.3:1	7.3:1
Bhp x rpm	45 @ 5300	45 @ 5300	55 @ 5700	55 @ 5700
Ignition	Lucas GQ coil All models			
Petrol tank	4 gallons All models			
Oil tank	5 pints All models			
Max speed	110 mph	110 mph	125 mph	125 mph
Weight	447 lb.	460 lb.	447 lb.	460 lb.
Wheelbase	56½ in. All models			
Tyres	Front – 3.50 x 19 Rear – 4.00 x 18			
Carburettor	Amal Monobloc 376 Amal Monobloc 389			